DC SUPER HERO GIRLS

FINALS CRISIS

an original graphic novel

WRITTEN BY **Shea Fontana**

ART BY **Yancey Labat**

COLORS BY **Monica Kubina**

LETTERING BY **Janice Chiang**

SUPERGIRL BASED ON THE CHARACTERS CREATED BY JERRY SIEGEL AND JOE SHUSTER. BY SPECIAL ARRANGEMENT WITH THE JERRY SIEGEL FAMILY.

MARIE JAVINS Editor
BRITTANY HOLZHERR Assistant Editor
STEVE COOK Design Director - Books
AMIE BROCKWAY-METCALF Publication Design

BOB HARRAS Senior VP - Editor-in-Chief, DC Comics

DIANE NELSON President
DAN DIDIO AND JIM LEE Co-Publishers
GEOFF JOHNS Chief Creative Officer
AMIT DESAI Senior VP - Marketing & Global Franchise Management
NAIRI GARDINER Senior VP - Finance
SAM ADES VP - Digital Marketing
BOBBIE CHASE VP - Talent Development
MARK CHIARELLO Senior VP - Art, Design & Collected Editions
JOHN CUNNINGHAM VP - Content Strategy
ANNE DEPIES VP - Strategy Planning & Reporting
DON FALLETTI VP - Manufacturing Operations
LAWRENCE GANEM VP - Editorial Administration & Talent Relations
ALISON GILL Senior VP - Manufacturing & Operations
HANK KANALZ Senior VP - Editorial Strategy & Administration
JAY KOGAN VP - Legal Affairs
DEREK MADDALENA Senior VP - Sales & Business Development
JACK MAHAN VP - Business Affairs
DAN MIRON VP - Sales Planning & Trade Development
NICK NAPOLITANO VP - Manufacturing Administration
CAROL ROEDER VP - Marketing
EDDIE SCANNELL VP - Mass Account & Digital Sales
COURTNEY SIMMONS Senior VP - Publicity & Communications
JIM (SKI) SOKOLOWSKI VP - Comic Book Specialty & Newsstand Sales
SANDY YI Senior VP - Global Franchise Management

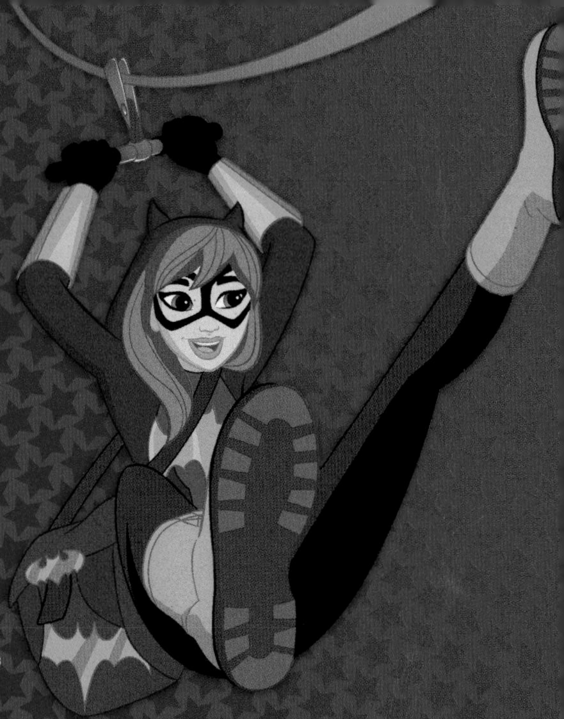

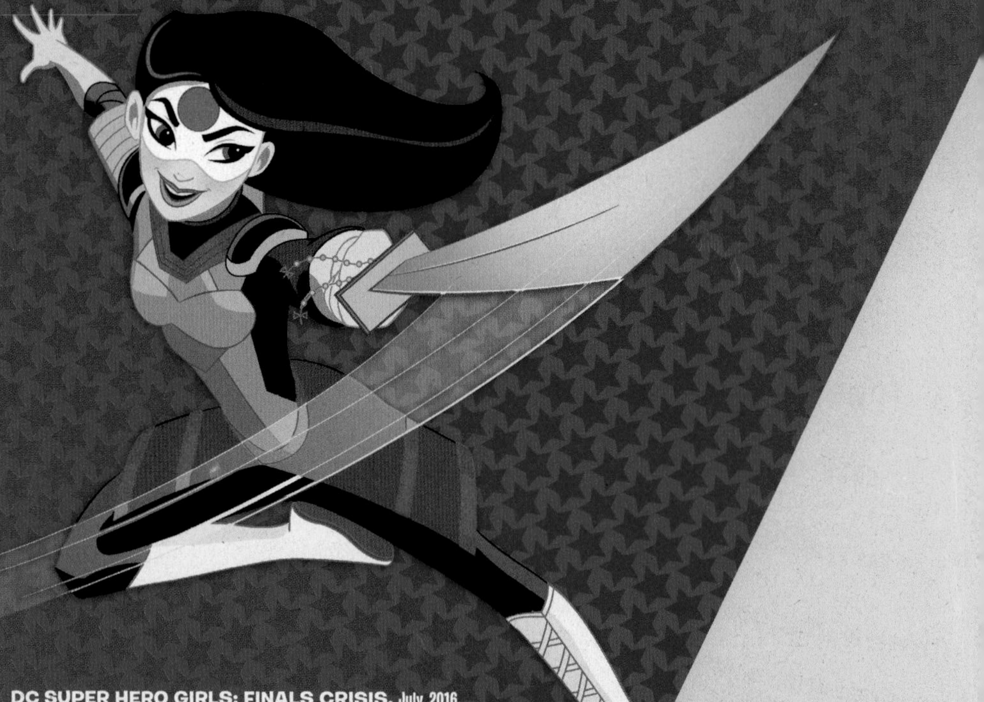

DC SUPER HERO GIRLS: FINALS CRISIS. July, 2016.
Published by DC Comics, 2900 W. Alameda Avenue, Burbank, CA 91505. GST # is R125921072.

This book is manufactured at a facility holding chain-of-custody certification. This paper is made with sustainably managed North American fiber. For Advertising and Custom Publishing contact dccomicsadvertising@dccomics.com. For details on DC Comics Ratings, visit dccomics.com/go/ratings.
Printed by Transcontinental Interglobe, Beauceville, QC, Canada. 5/6/16. ISBN: 978-1-4012-7021-6

PEFC Certified
Printed on paper from sustainably managed forests and controlled sources
PEFC
PEFC/01-31-106
www.pefc.org

TABLE OF CONTENTS

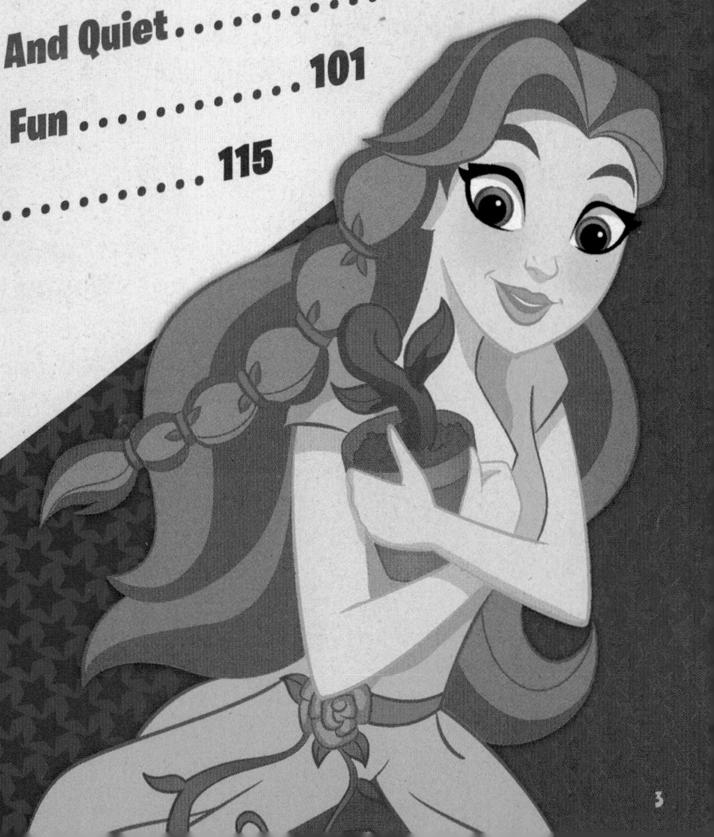

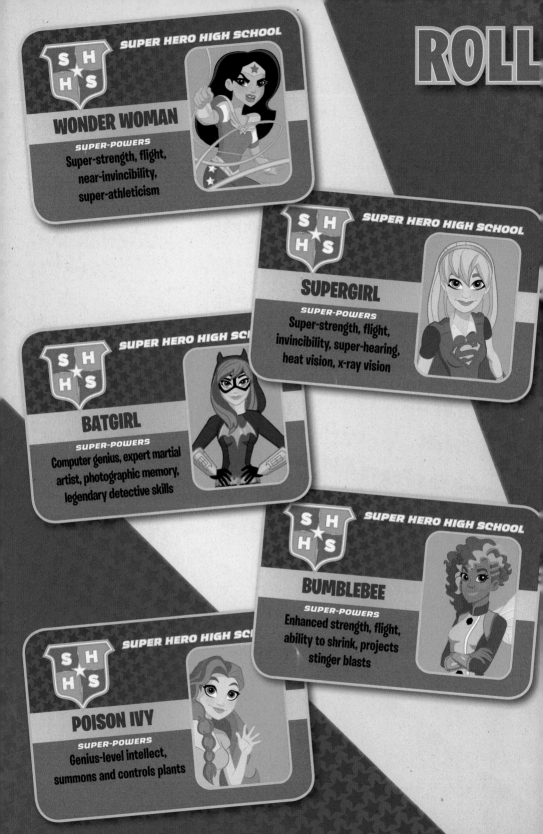

SUPER HERO HIGH SCHOOL

WONDER WOMAN

SUPER-POWERS
Super-strength, flight, near-invincibility, super-athleticism

SUPER HERO HIGH SCHOOL

SUPERGIRL

SUPER-POWERS
Super-strength, flight, invincibility, super-hearing, heat vision, x-ray vision

SUPER HERO HIGH SCHOOL

BATGIRL

SUPER-POWERS
Computer genius, expert martial artist, photographic memory, legendary detective skills

SUPER HERO HIGH SCHOOL

BUMBLEBEE

SUPER-POWERS
Enhanced strength, flight, ability to shrink, projects stinger blasts

SUPER HERO HIGH SCHOOL

POISON IVY

SUPER-POWERS
Genius-level intellect, summons and controls plants

CALL

SUPER HERO HIGH SCHOOL

SHHS

HARLEY QUINN

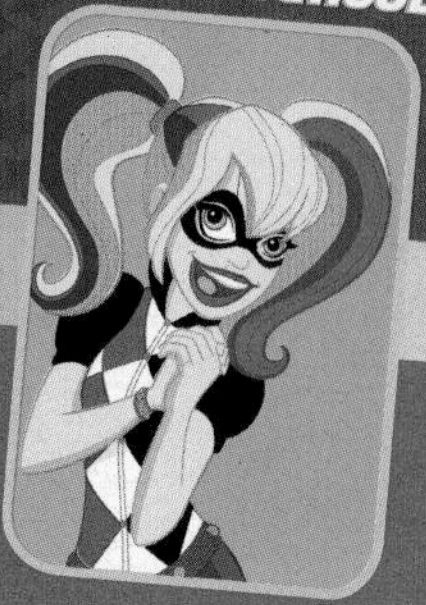

SUPER-POWERS

Expert gymnast, acrobat, quick-witted class clown

SUPER HERO HIGH SCHOOL

SHHS

KATANA

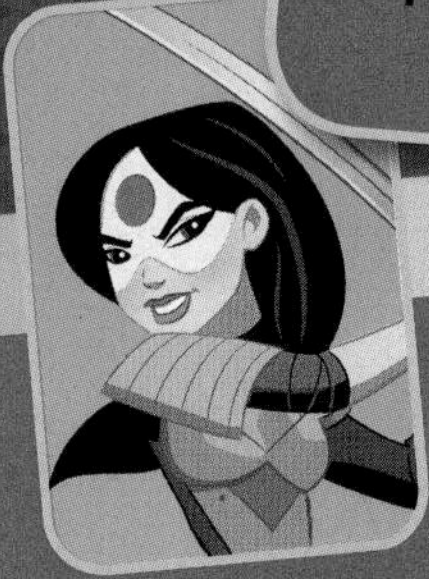

SUPER-POWERS

Champion Samurai sword fighter, expert martial artist, painter

SUPER HERO HIGH SCHOOL

SHHS

BEAST BOY

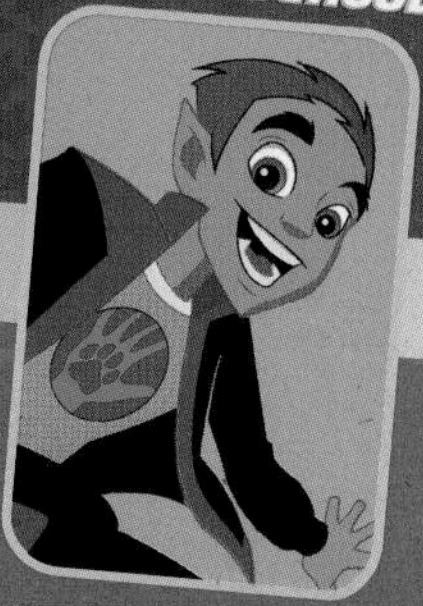

SUPER-POWERS

Shape shifts into any animal form, world-class slacker

SUPER HERO HIGH SCHOOL

SHHS

AMANDA WALLER

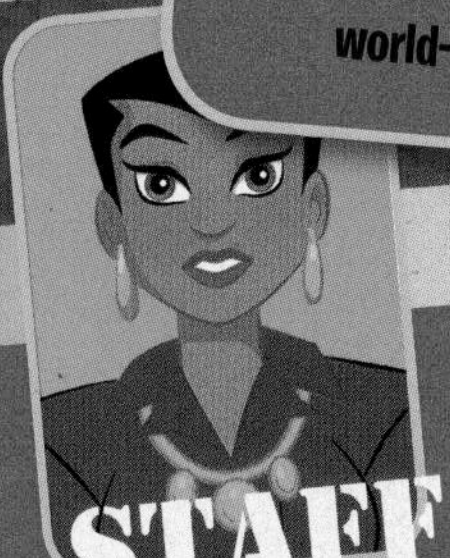
STAFF

Principal

SUPER HERO HIGH SCHOOL

SHHS

GORILLA GRODD

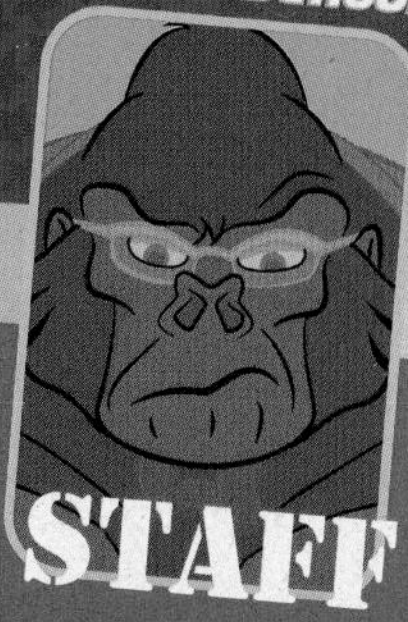
STAFF

Vice-principal

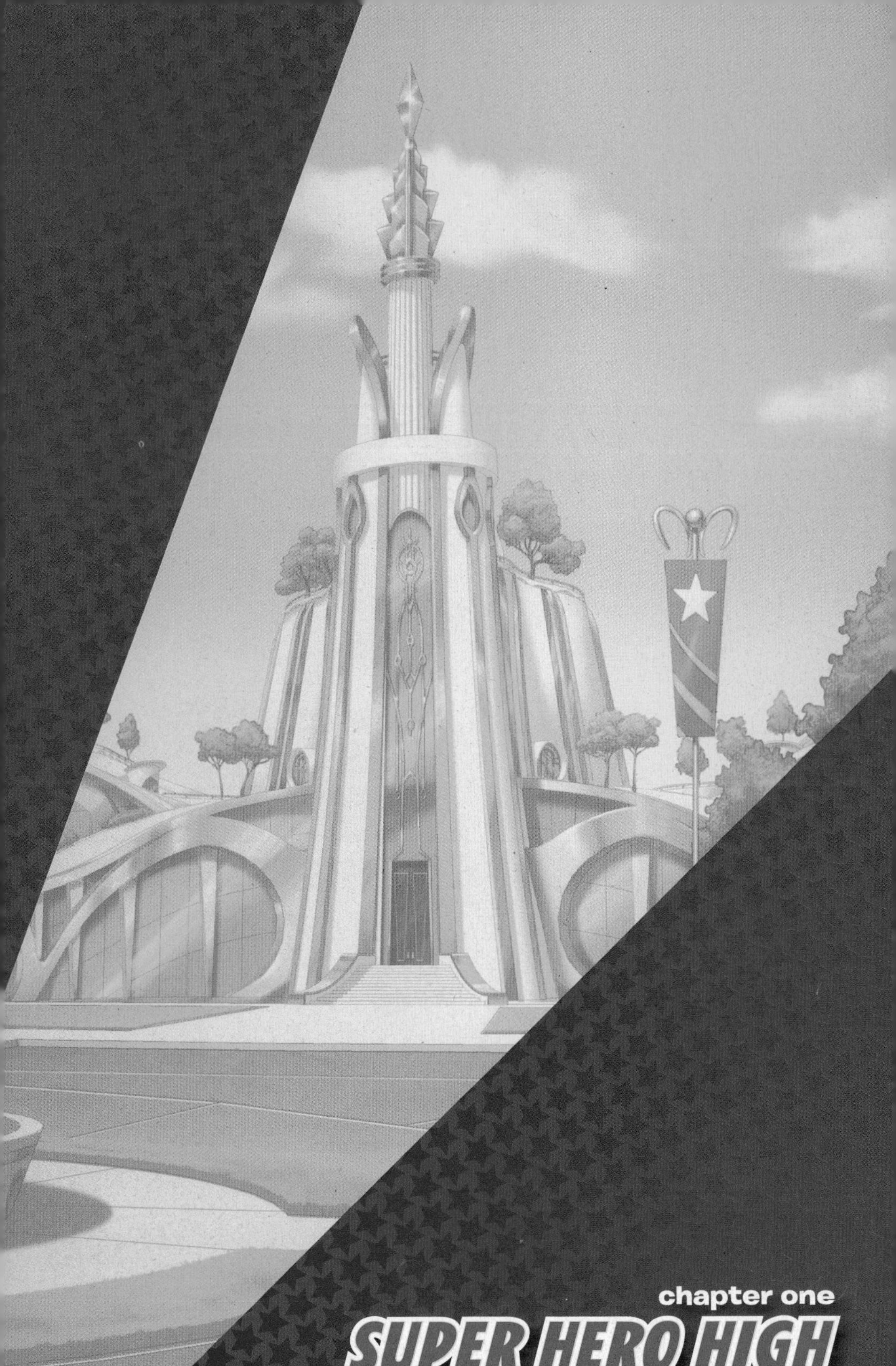

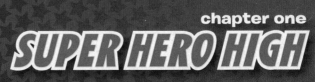

chapter one

SUPER HERO HIGH

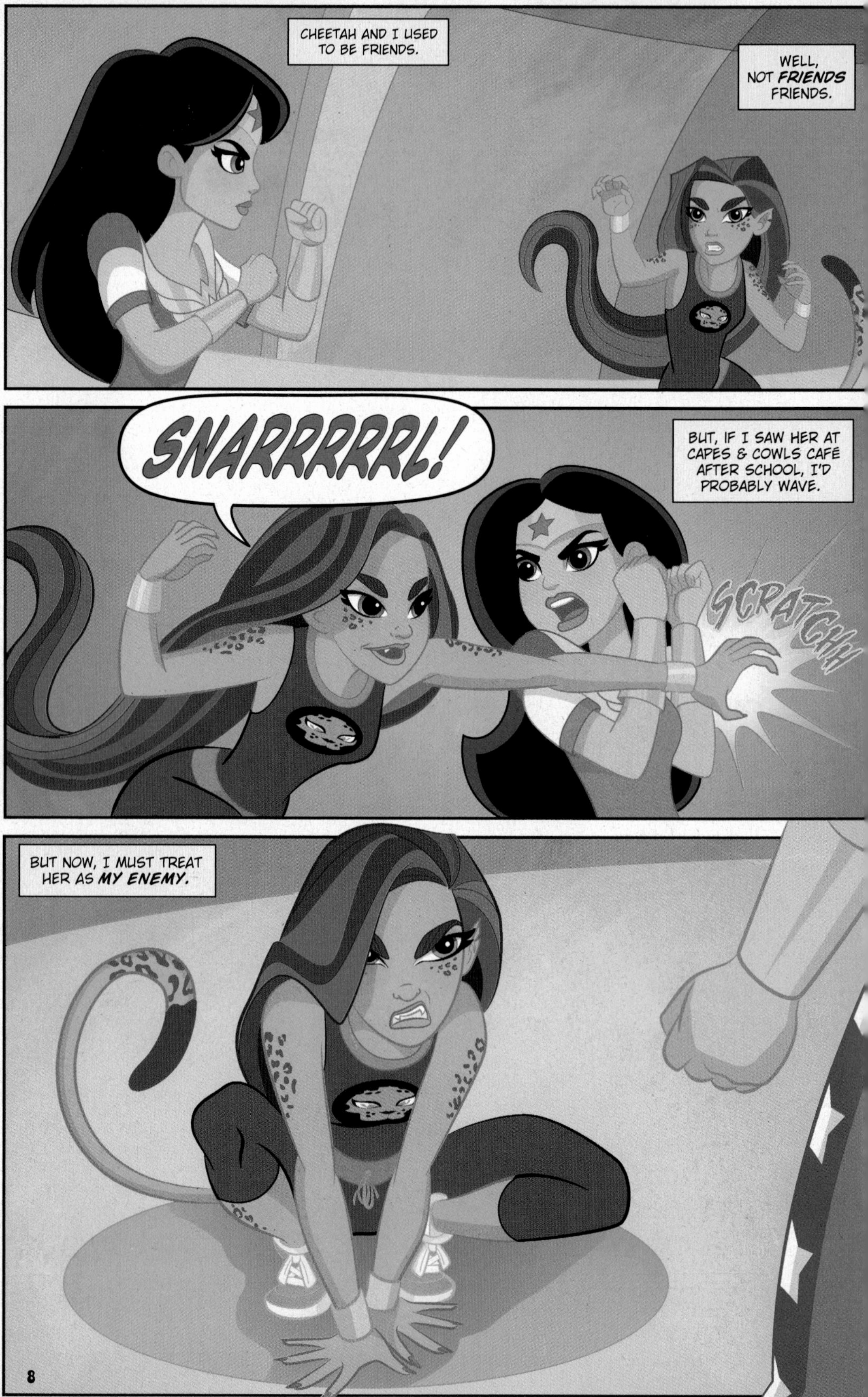
CHEETAH AND I USED TO BE FRIENDS.
WELL, NOT FRIENDS FRIENDS.
SNARRRRRRL!
BUT, IF I SAW HER AT CAPES & COWLS CAFÉ AFTER SCHOOL, I'D PROBABLY WAVE.
SCRATCHH
BUT NOW, I MUST TREAT HER AS MY ENEMY.

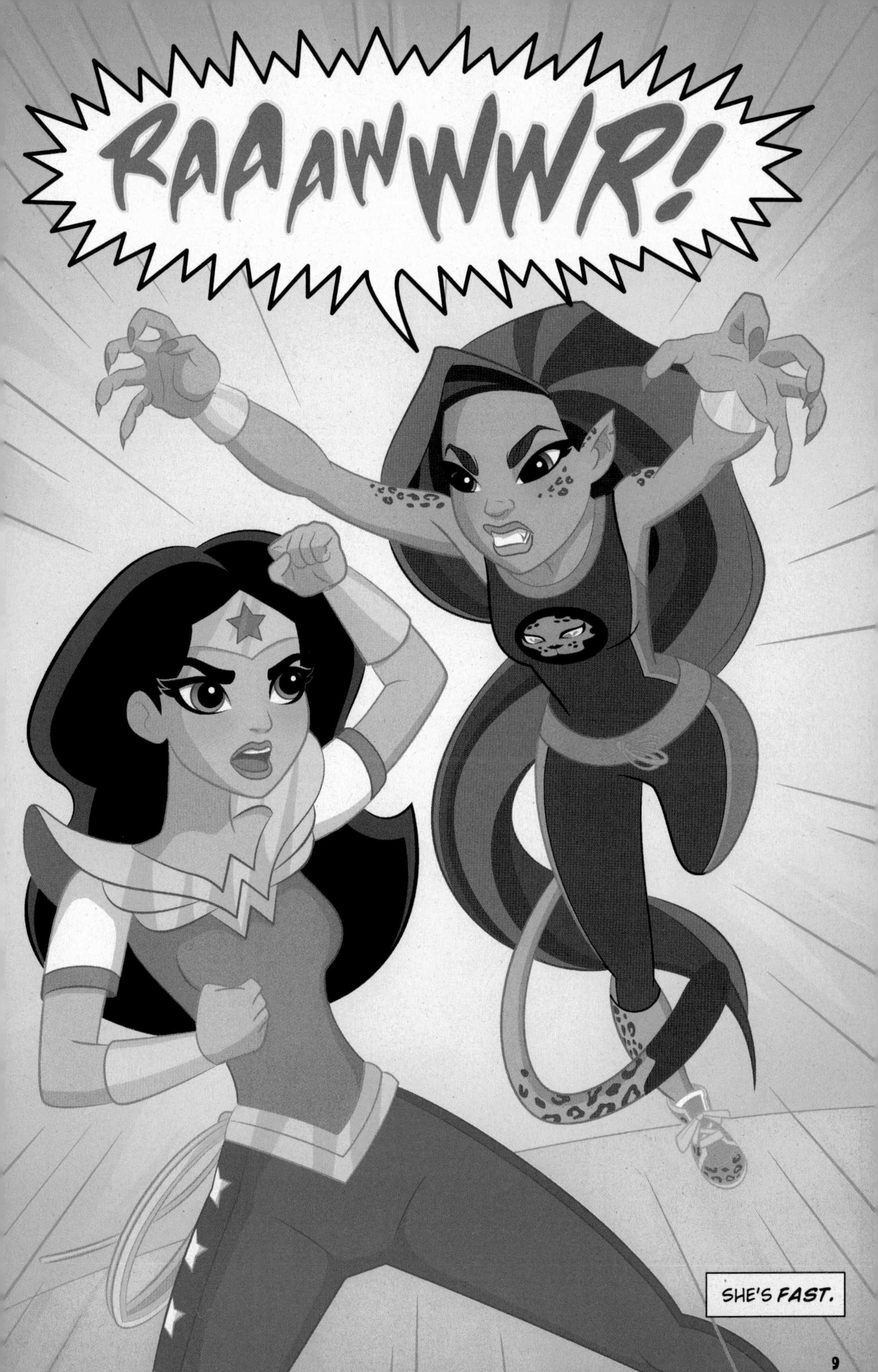
RAAAWWWR!
SHE'S FAST.

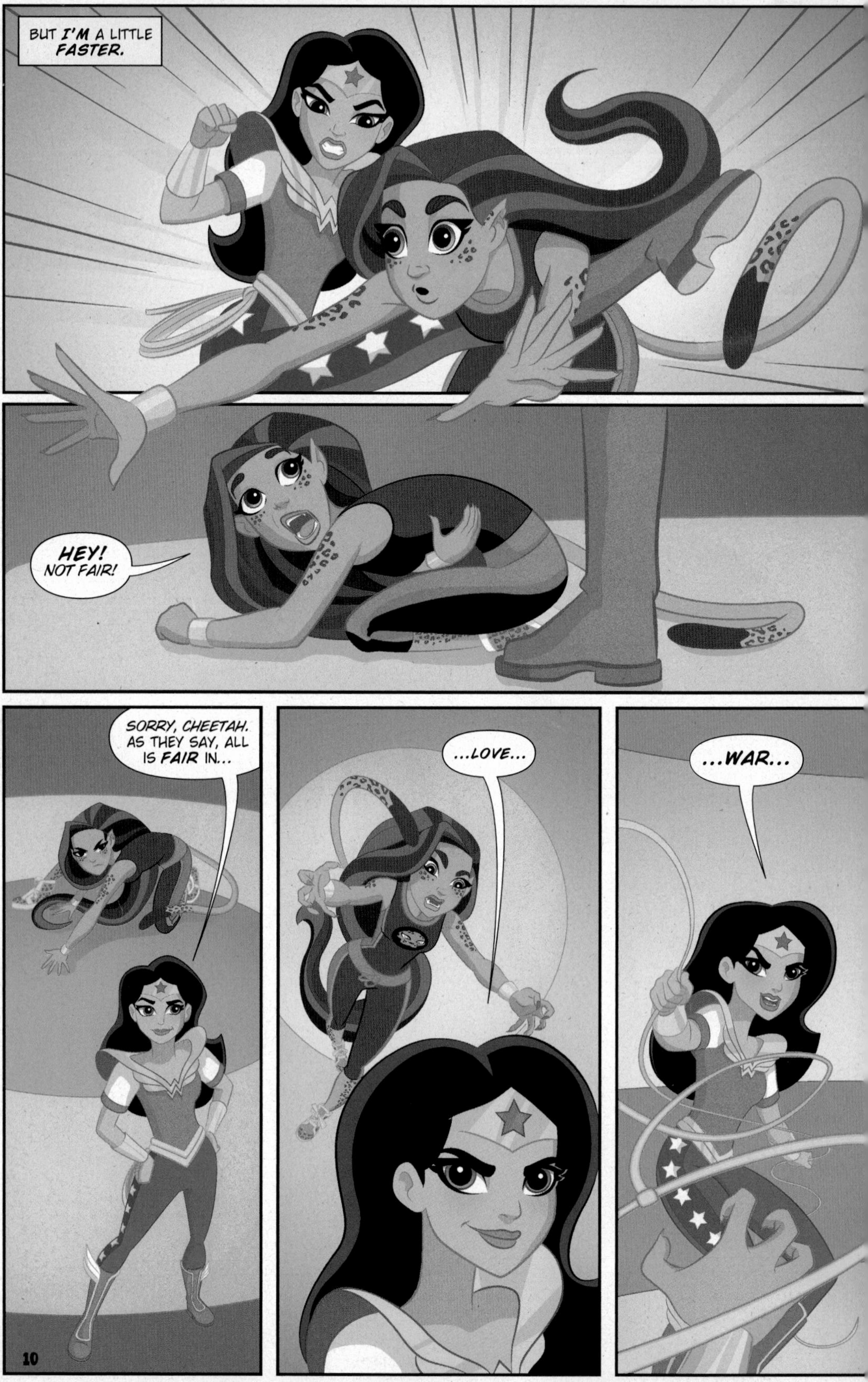
BUT I'M A LITTLE FASTER.
HEY! NOT FAIR!
SORRY, CHEETAH. AS THEY SAY, ALL IS FAIR IN...
...LOVE...
...WAR...

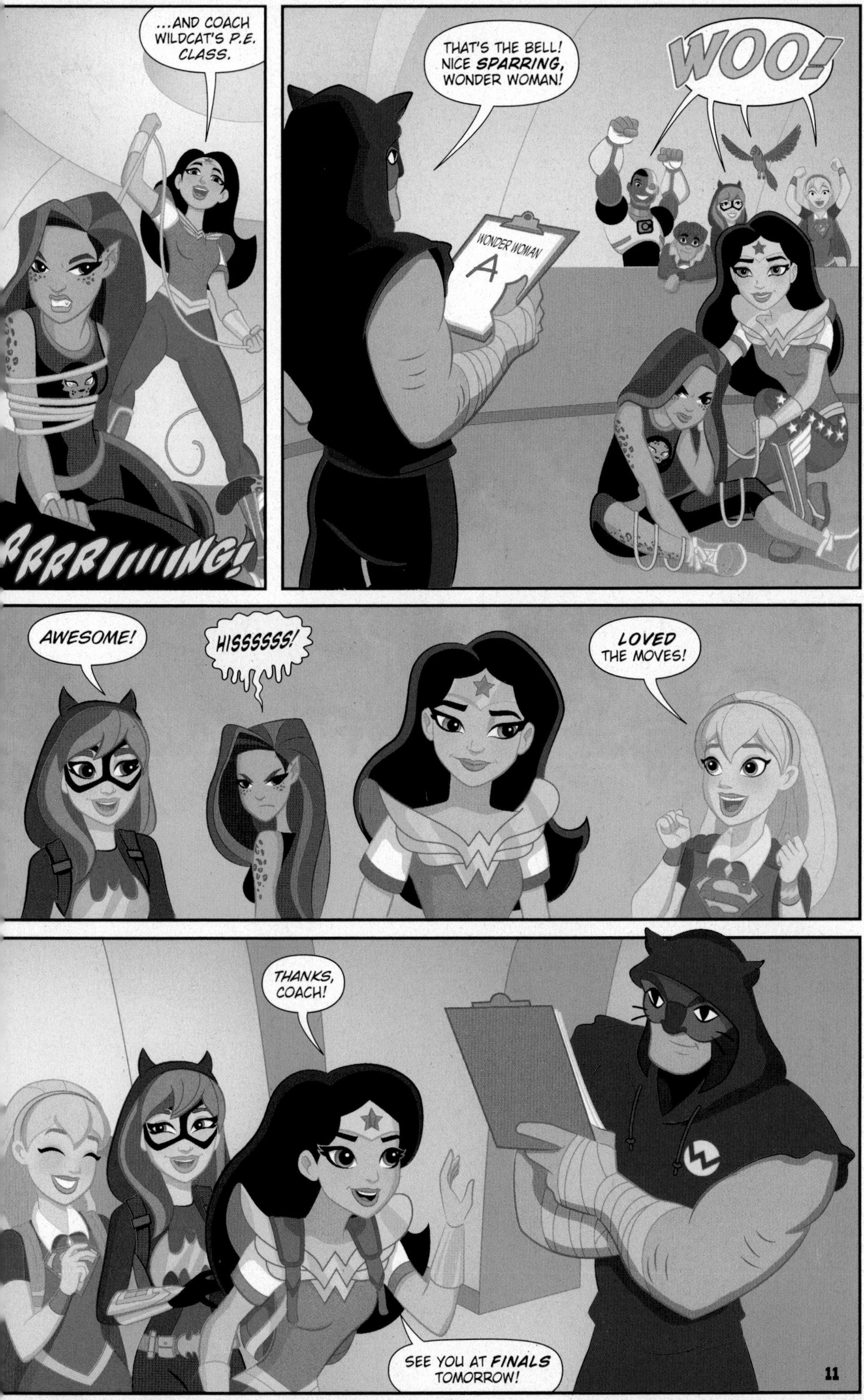
...AND COACH WILDCAT'S P.E. CLASS.
RRRRIIIIING!
THAT'S THE BELL! NICE SPARRING, WONDER WOMAN!
WONDER WOMAN A
WOO!
AWESOME!
HISSSSSS!
LOVED THE MOVES!
THANKS, COACH!
SEE YOU AT FINALS TOMORROW!

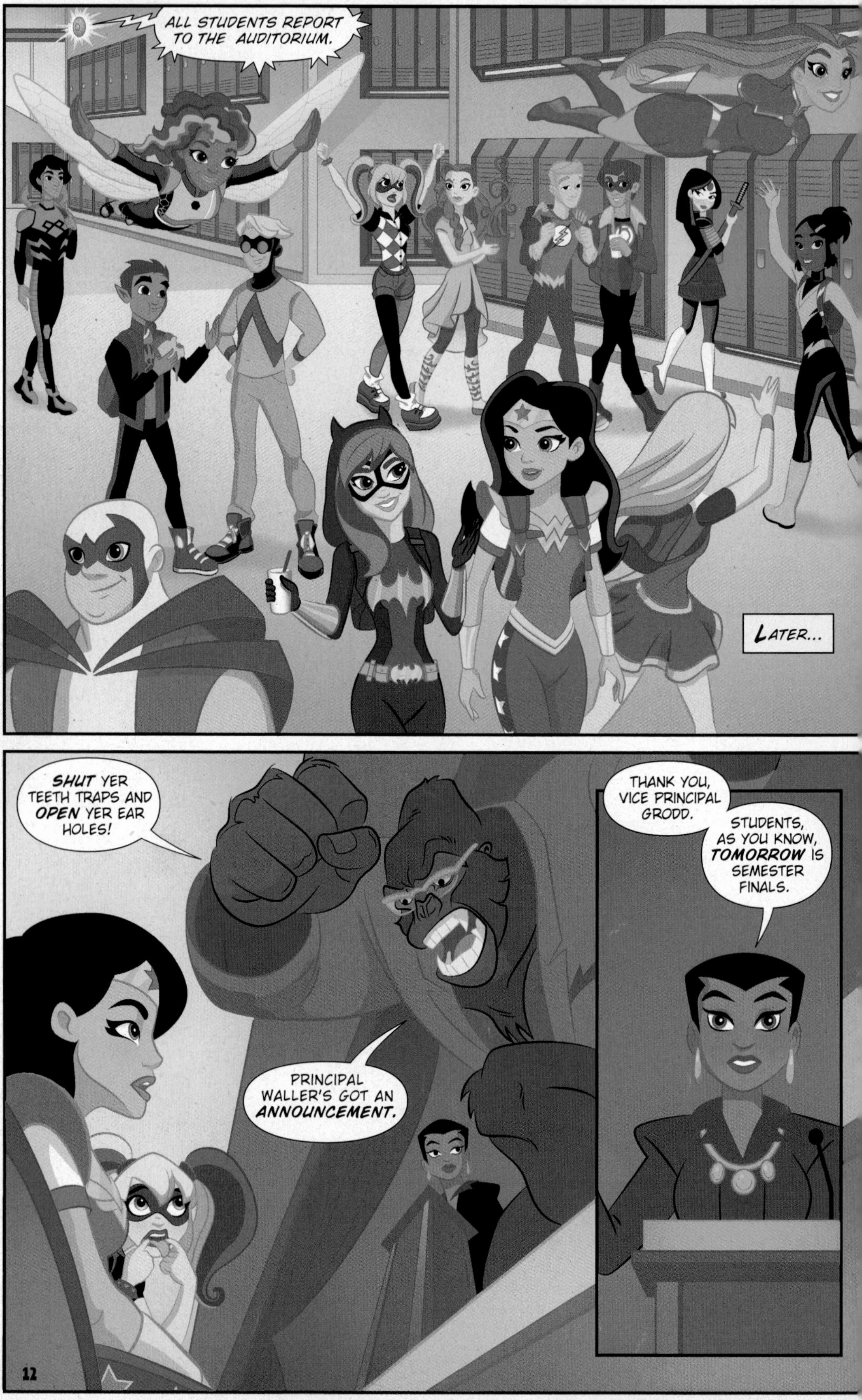

ALL STUDENTS REPORT TO THE AUDITORIUM.
LATER...
SHUT YER TEETH TRAPS AND OPEN YER EAR HOLES!
PRINCIPAL WALLER'S GOT AN ANNOUNCEMENT.
THANK YOU, VICE PRINCIPAL GRODD.
STUDENTS, AS YOU KNOW, TOMORROW IS SEMESTER FINALS.

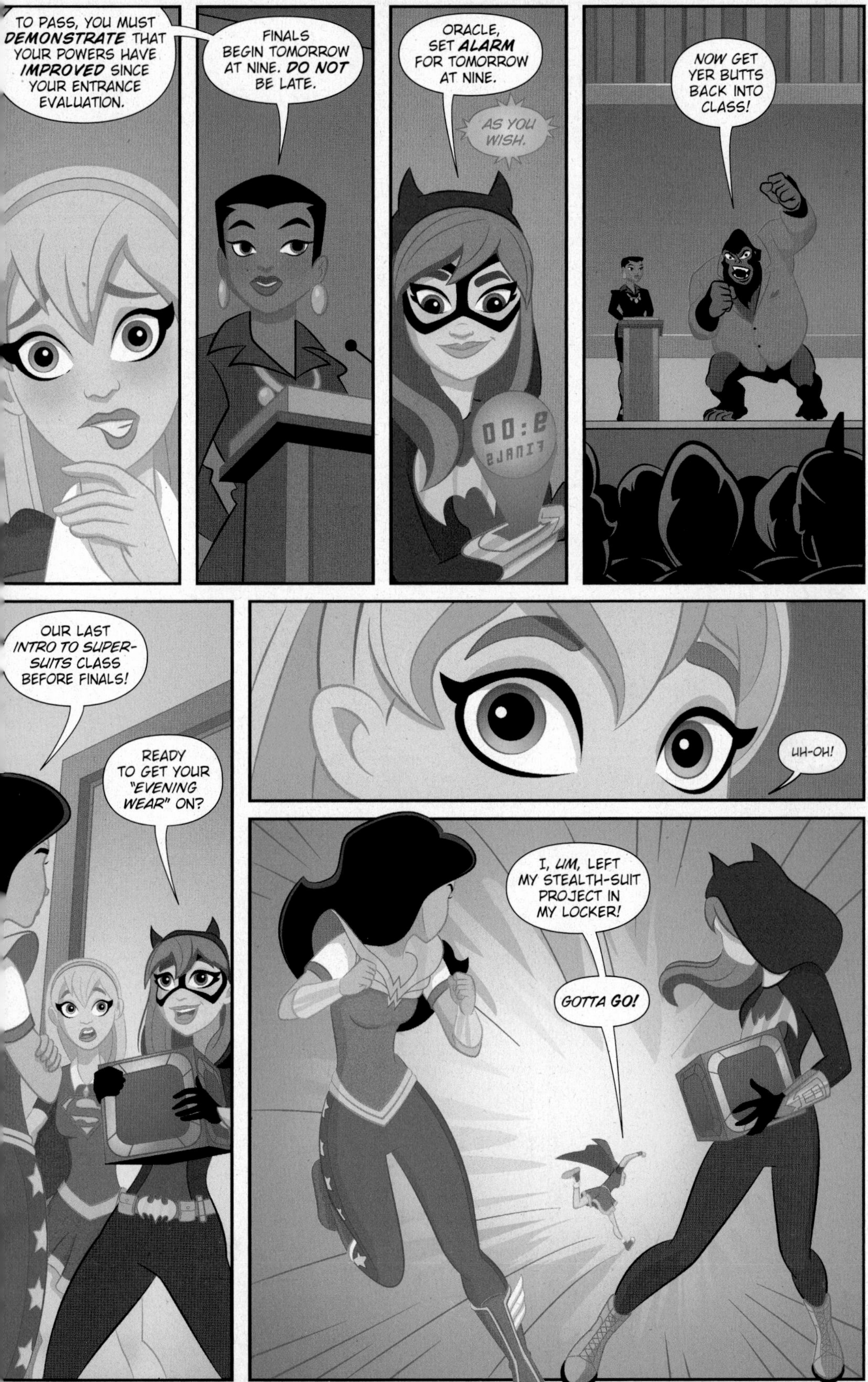
TO PASS, YOU MUST DEMONSTRATE THAT YOUR POWERS HAVE IMPROVED SINCE YOUR ENTRANCE EVALUATION.
FINALS BEGIN TOMORROW AT NINE. DO NOT BE LATE.
ORACLE, SET ALARM FOR TOMORROW AT NINE.
AS YOU WISH.
NOW GET YER BUTTS BACK INTO CLASS!
OUR LAST INTRO TO SUPER-SUITS CLASS BEFORE FINALS!
READY TO GET YOUR "EVENING WEAR" ON?
UH-OH!
I, UM, LEFT MY STEALTH-SUIT PROJECT IN MY LOCKER!
GOTTA GO!

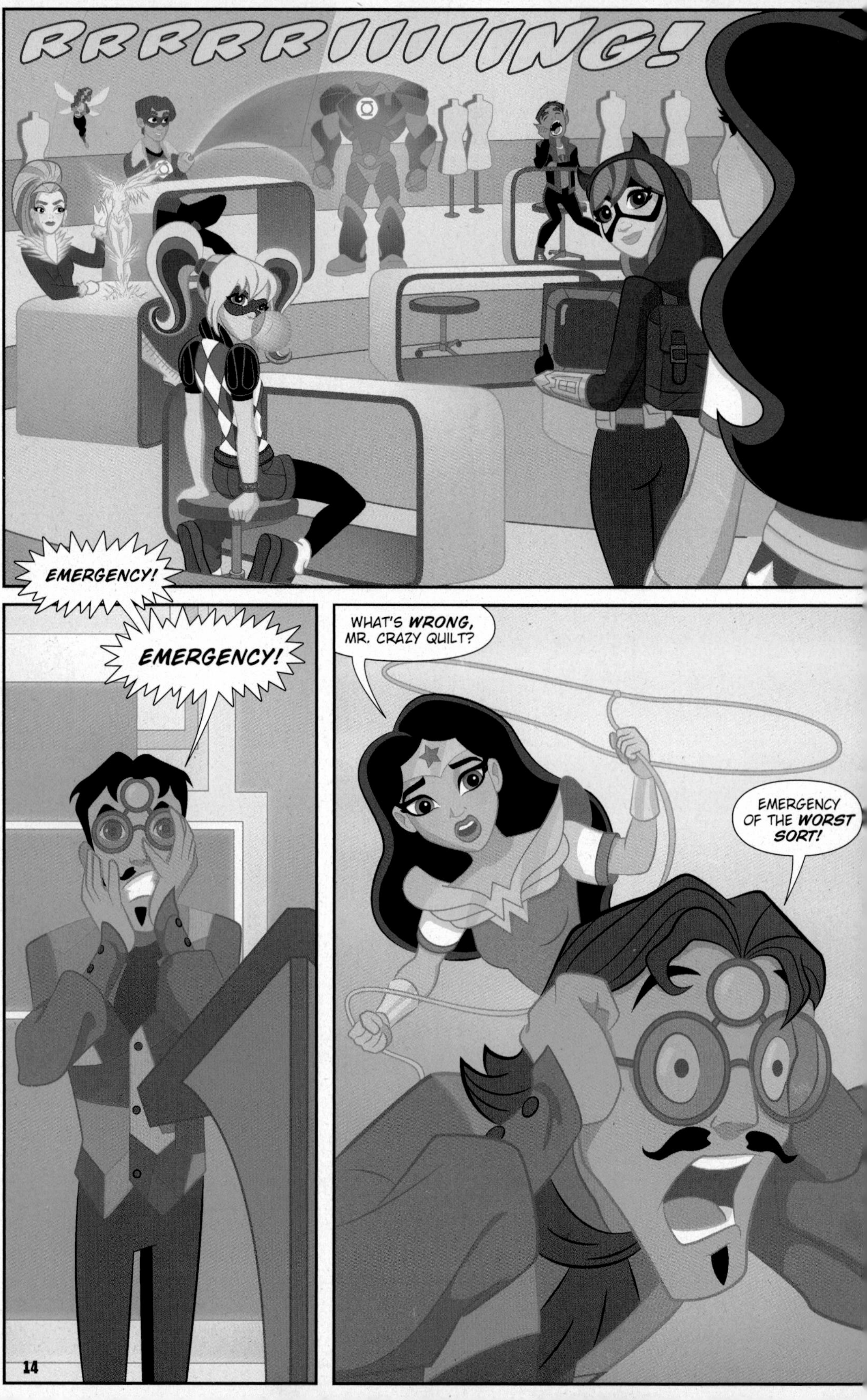
RRRRRIIIIING!
EMERGENCY!
EMERGENCY!
WHAT'S **WRONG**, MR. CRAZY QUILT?
EMERGENCY OF THE **WORST** SORT!

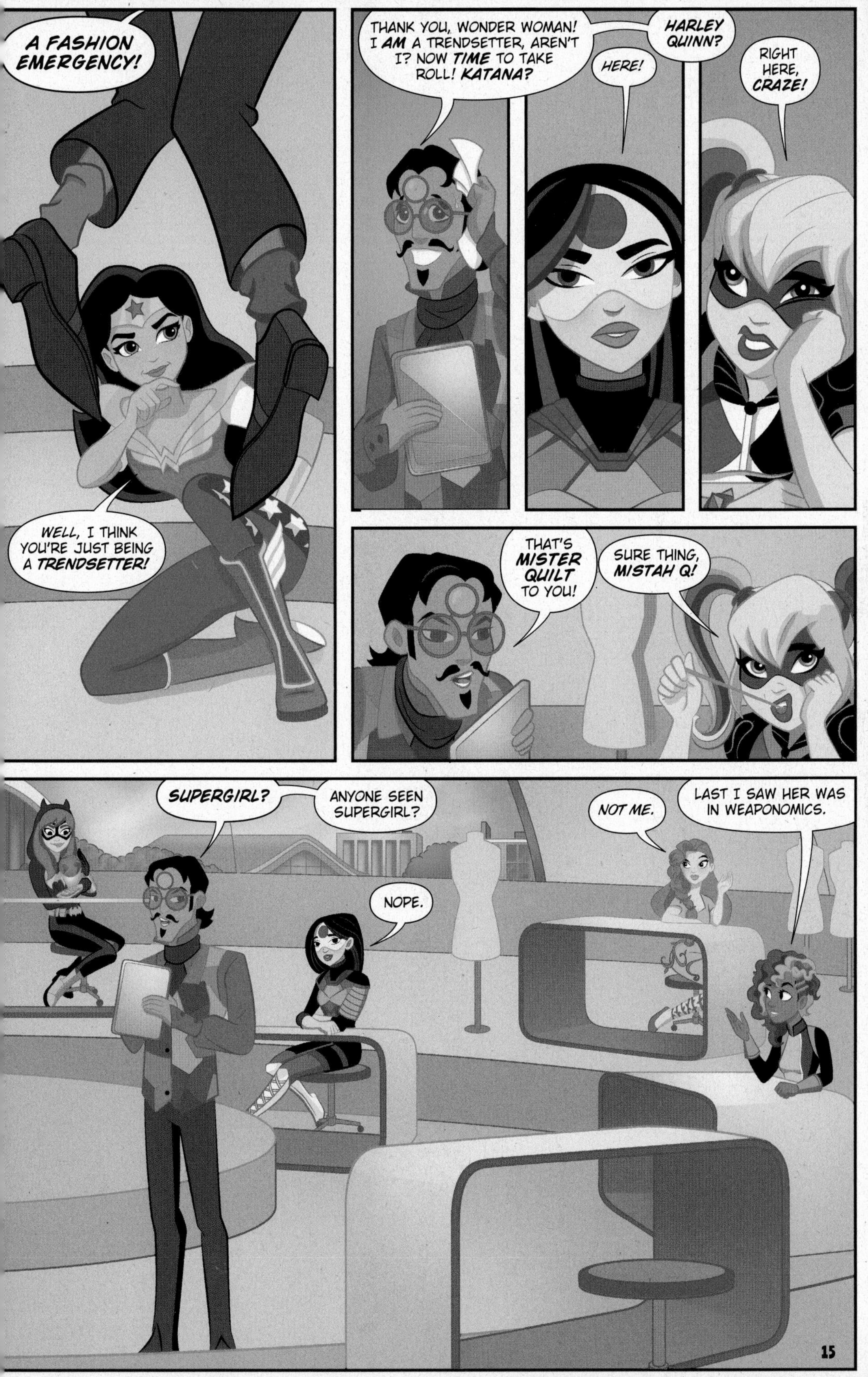

A FASHION EMERGENCY!
WELL, I THINK YOU'RE JUST BEING A TRENDSETTER!
THANK YOU, WONDER WOMAN! I AM A TRENDSETTER, AREN'T I? NOW TIME TO TAKE ROLL! KATANA?
HERE!
HARLEY QUINN?
RIGHT HERE, CRAZE!
THAT'S MISTER QUILT TO YOU!
SURE THING, MISTAH Q!
SUPERGIRL?
ANYONE SEEN SUPERGIRL?
NOPE.
NOT ME.
LAST I SAW HER WAS IN WEAPONOMICS.

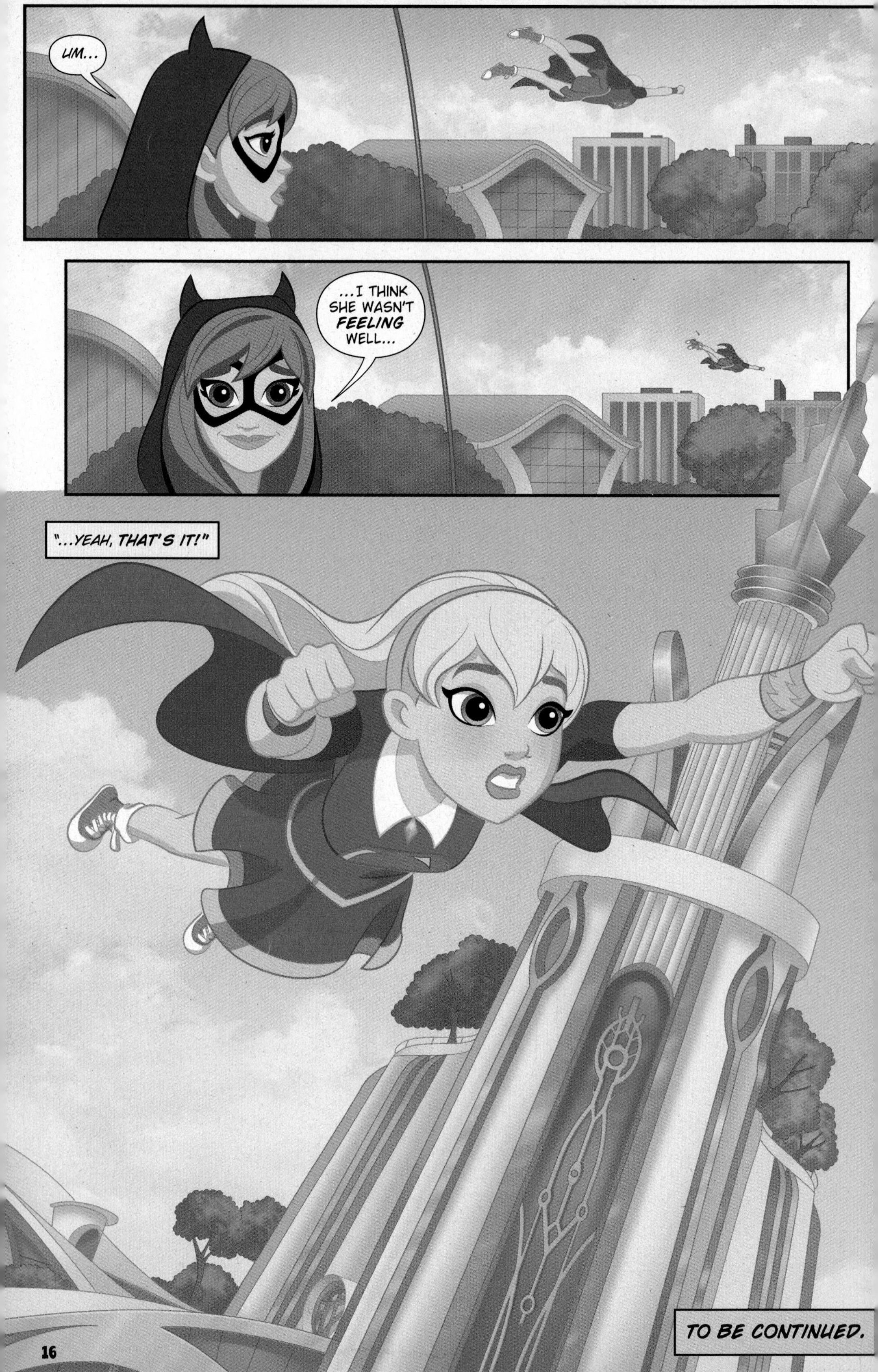
UM...
...I THINK SHE WASN'T FEELING WELL...
"...YEAH, THAT'S IT!"
TO BE CONTINUED.

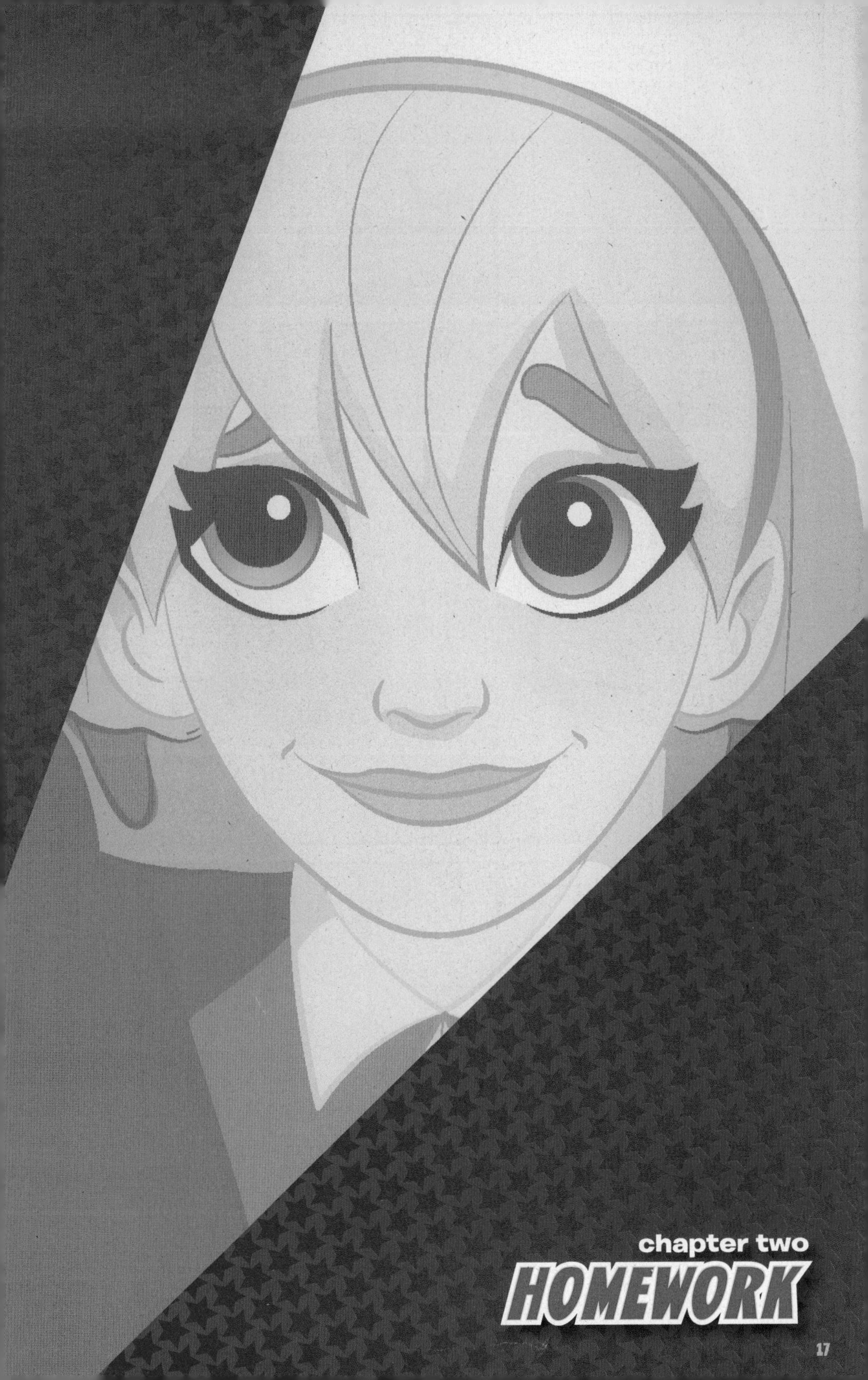

chapter two

HOMEWORK

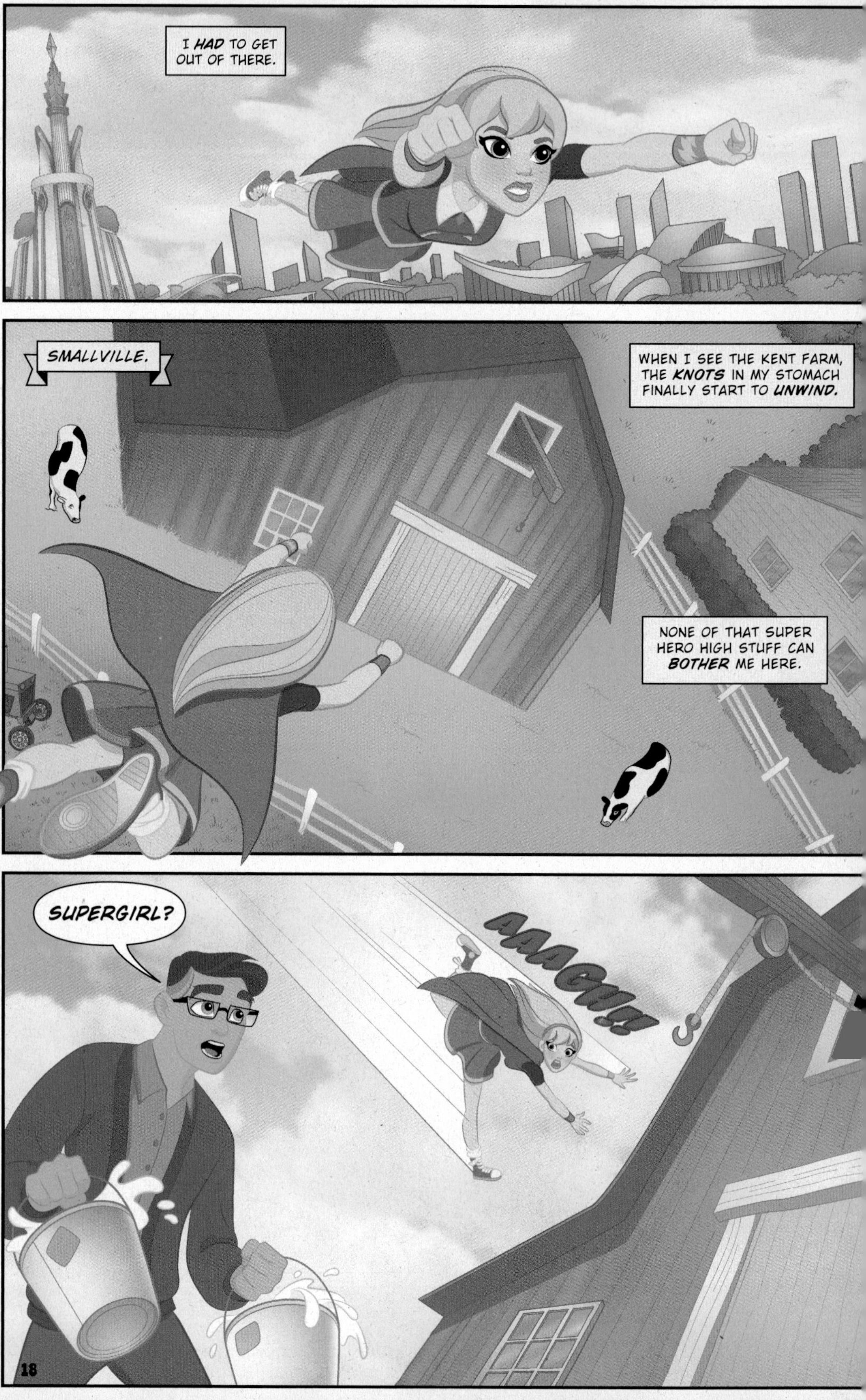
I HAD TO GET OUT OF THERE.
SMALLVILLE.
WHEN I SEE THE KENT FARM, THE KNOTS IN MY STOMACH FINALLY START TO UNWIND.
NONE OF THAT SUPER HERO HIGH STUFF CAN BOTHER ME HERE.
SUPERGIRL?
AAACH!!

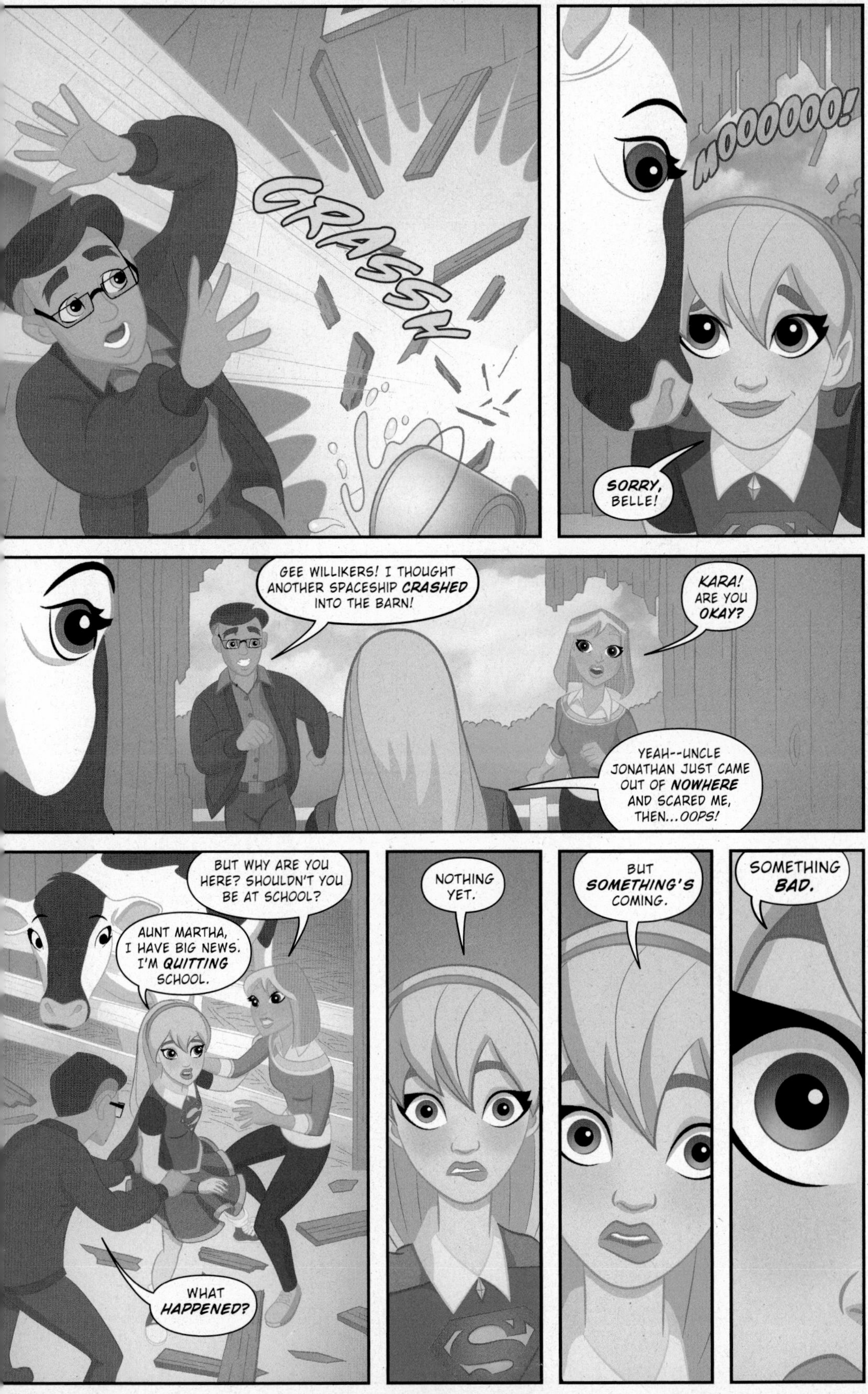

CRASSH
MOOOOOO!
SORRY, BELLE!
GEE WILLIKERS! I THOUGHT ANOTHER SPACESHIP CRASHED INTO THE BARN!
KARA! ARE YOU OKAY?
YEAH--UNCLE JONATHAN JUST CAME OUT OF NOWHERE AND SCARED ME, THEN...OOPS!
BUT WHY ARE YOU HERE? SHOULDN'T YOU BE AT SCHOOL?
AUNT MARTHA, I HAVE BIG NEWS. I'M QUITTING SCHOOL.
WHAT HAPPENED?
NOTHING YET.
BUT SOMETHING'S COMING.
SOMETHING BAD.

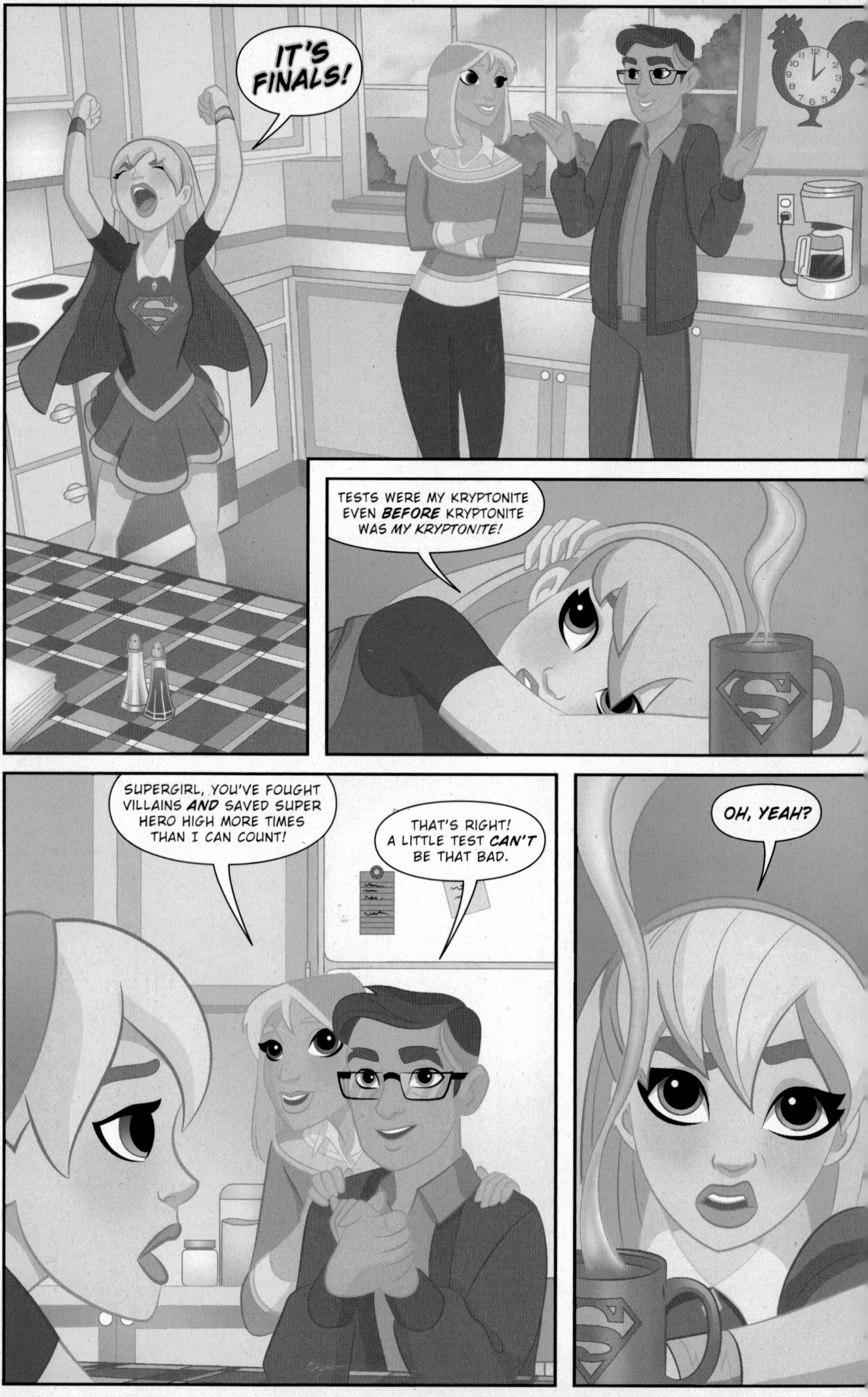
IT'S FINALS!
TESTS WERE MY KRYPTONITE EVEN BEFORE KRYPTONITE WAS MY KRYPTONITE!
SUPERGIRL, YOU'VE FOUGHT VILLAINS AND SAVED SUPER HERO HIGH MORE TIMES THAN I CAN COUNT!
THAT'S RIGHT! A LITTLE TEST CAN'T BE THAT BAD.
OH, YEAH?

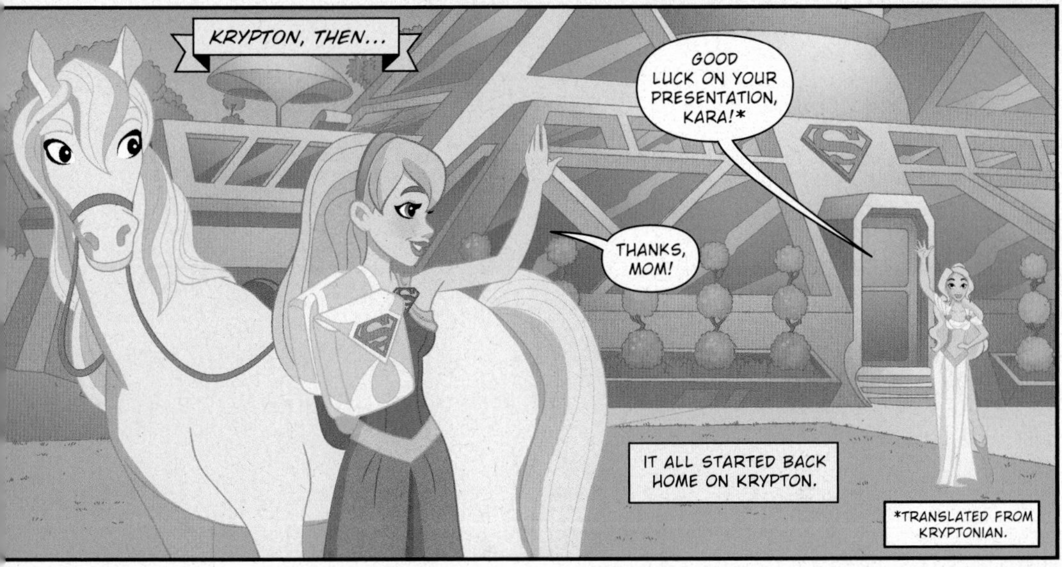
KRYPTON, THEN...
GOOD LUCK ON YOUR PRESENTATION, KARA!*
THANKS, MOM!
IT ALL STARTED BACK HOME ON KRYPTON.
*TRANSLATED FROM KRYPTONIAN.

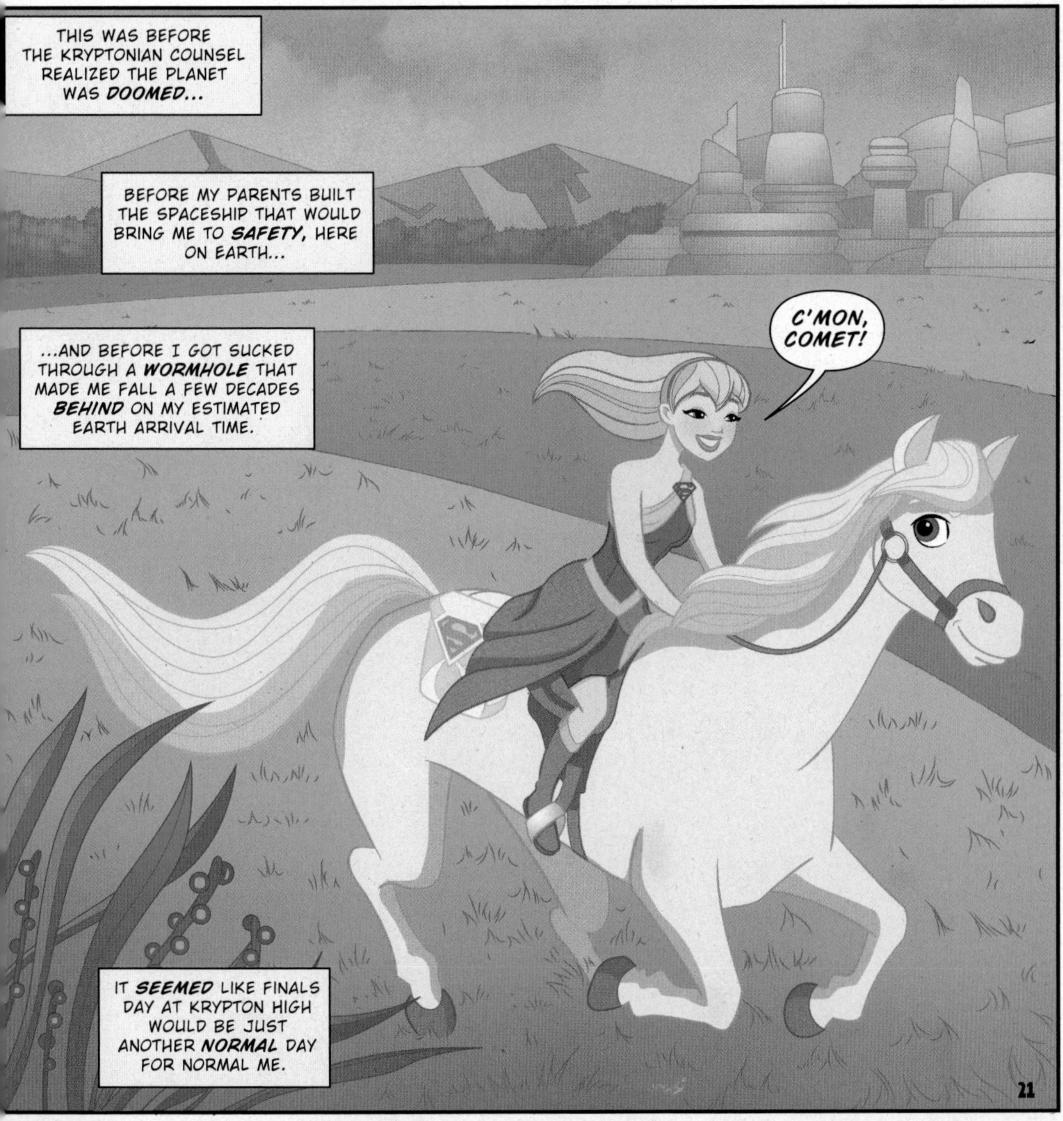
THIS WAS BEFORE THE KRYPTONIAN COUNSEL REALIZED THE PLANET WAS DOOMED...
BEFORE MY PARENTS BUILT THE SPACESHIP THAT WOULD BRING ME TO SAFETY, HERE ON EARTH...
...AND BEFORE I GOT SUCKED THROUGH A WORMHOLE THAT MADE ME FALL A FEW DECADES BEHIND ON MY ESTIMATED EARTH ARRIVAL TIME.
C'MON, COMET!
IT SEEMED LIKE FINALS DAY AT KRYPTON HIGH WOULD BE JUST ANOTHER NORMAL DAY FOR NORMAL ME.

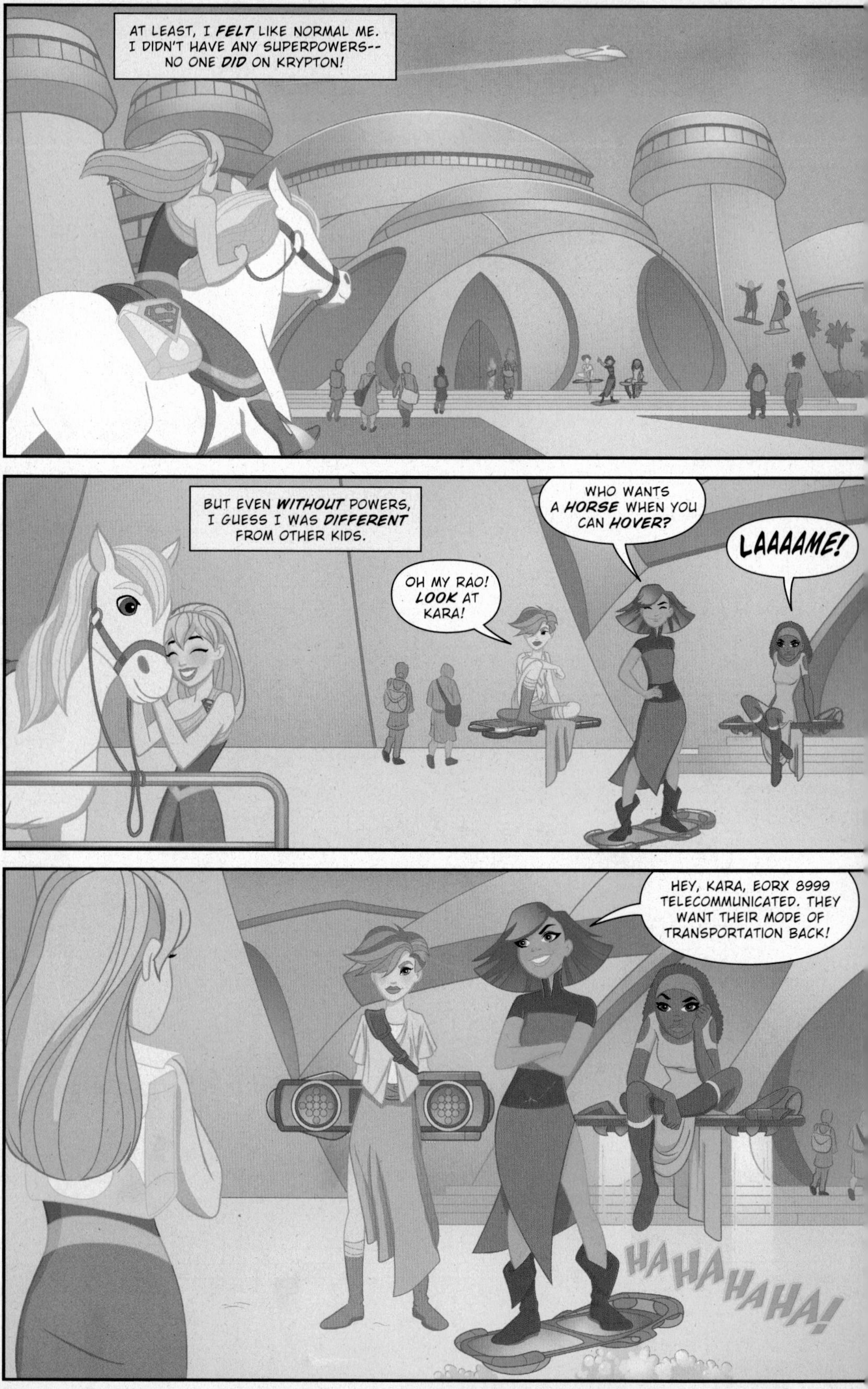
AT LEAST, I FELT LIKE NORMAL ME. I DIDN'T HAVE ANY SUPERPOWERS-- NO ONE DID ON KRYPTON!
BUT EVEN WITHOUT POWERS, I GUESS I WAS DIFFERENT FROM OTHER KIDS.
OH MY RAO! LOOK AT KARA!
WHO WANTS A HORSE WHEN YOU CAN HOVER?
LAAAAME!
HEY, KARA, EORX 8999 TELECOMMUNICATED. THEY WANT THEIR MODE OF TRANSPORTATION BACK!
HAHAHAHA!

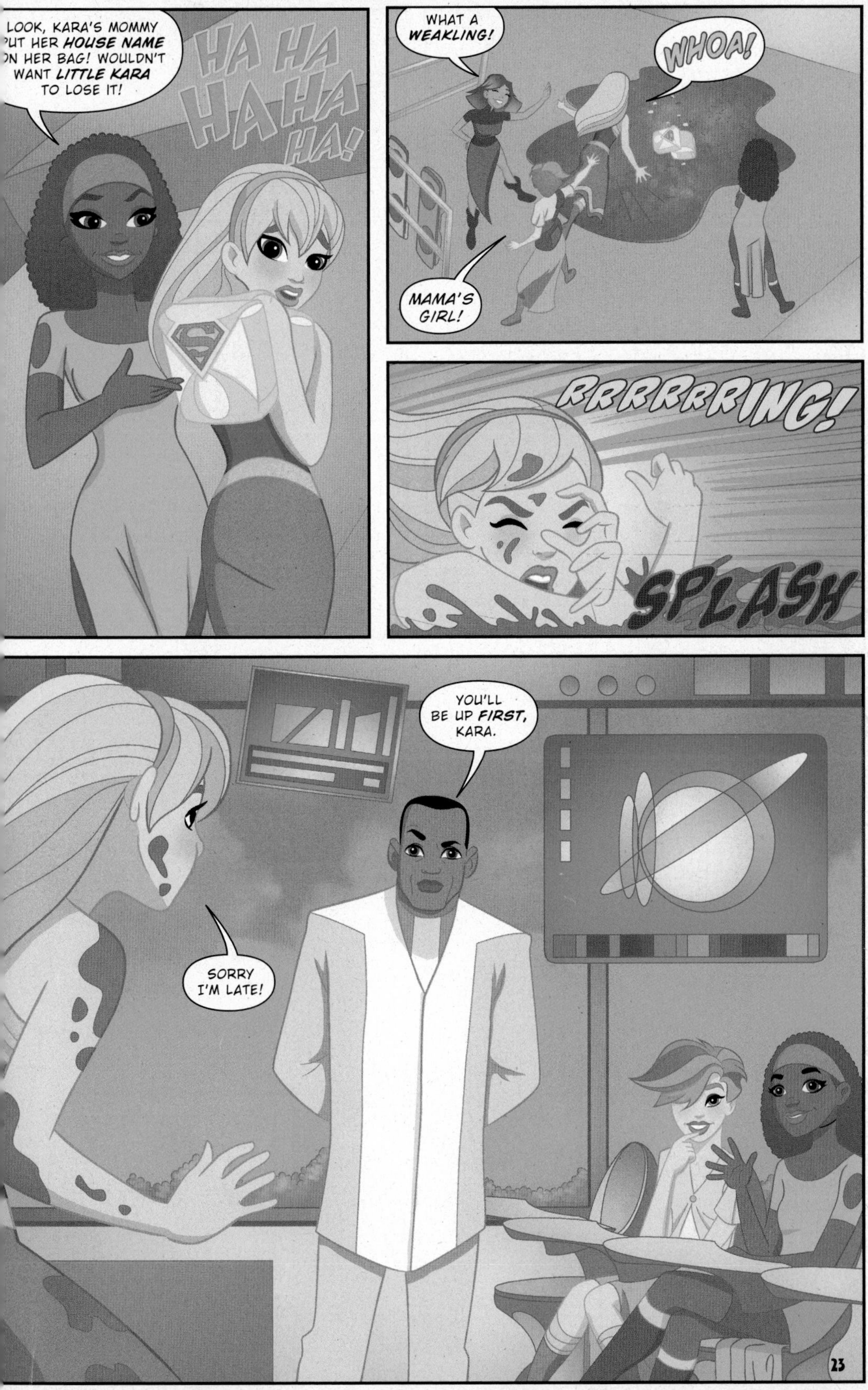

LOOK, KARA'S MOMMY PUT HER **HOUSE NAME** ON HER BAG! WOULDN'T WANT **LITTLE KARA** TO LOSE IT!
HA HA HA HA HA!
WHAT A **WEAKLING!**
WHOA!
MAMA'S GIRL!
RRRRRRING!
SPLASH
YOU'LL BE UP **FIRST,** KARA.
SORRY I'M LATE!

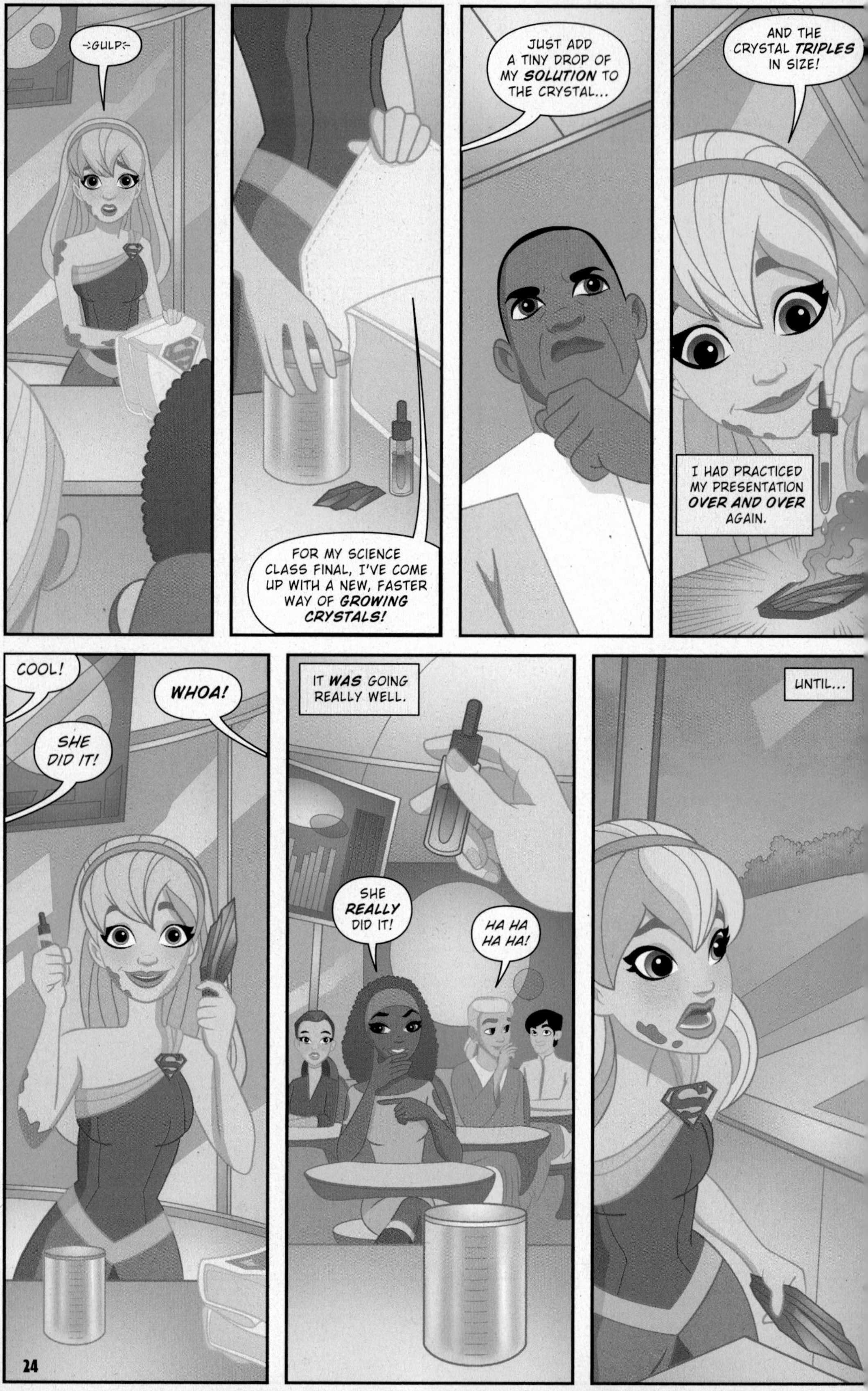

-GULP-
FOR MY SCIENCE CLASS FINAL, I'VE COME UP WITH A NEW, FASTER WAY OF GROWING CRYSTALS!
JUST ADD A TINY DROP OF MY SOLUTION TO THE CRYSTAL...
AND THE CRYSTAL TRIPLES IN SIZE!
I HAD PRACTICED MY PRESENTATION OVER AND OVER AGAIN.
COOL!
WHOA!
SHE DID IT!
IT WAS GOING REALLY WELL.
SHE REALLY DID IT!
HA HA HA HA!
UNTIL...

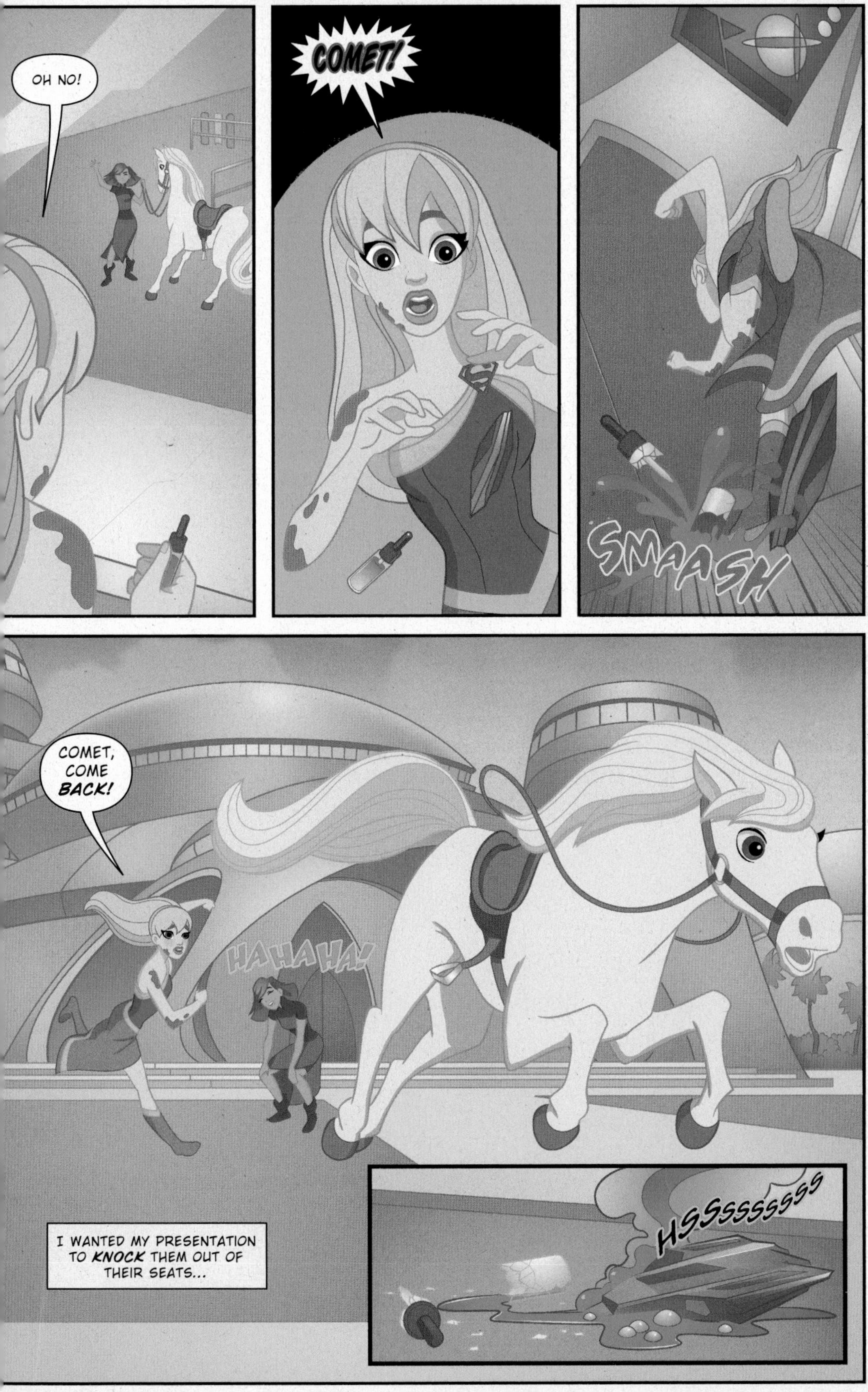
OH NO!
COMET!
SMAASH
COMET, COME BACK!
HAHAHA!
I WANTED MY PRESENTATION TO KNOCK THEM OUT OF THEIR SEATS...
HSSSSSSSSS

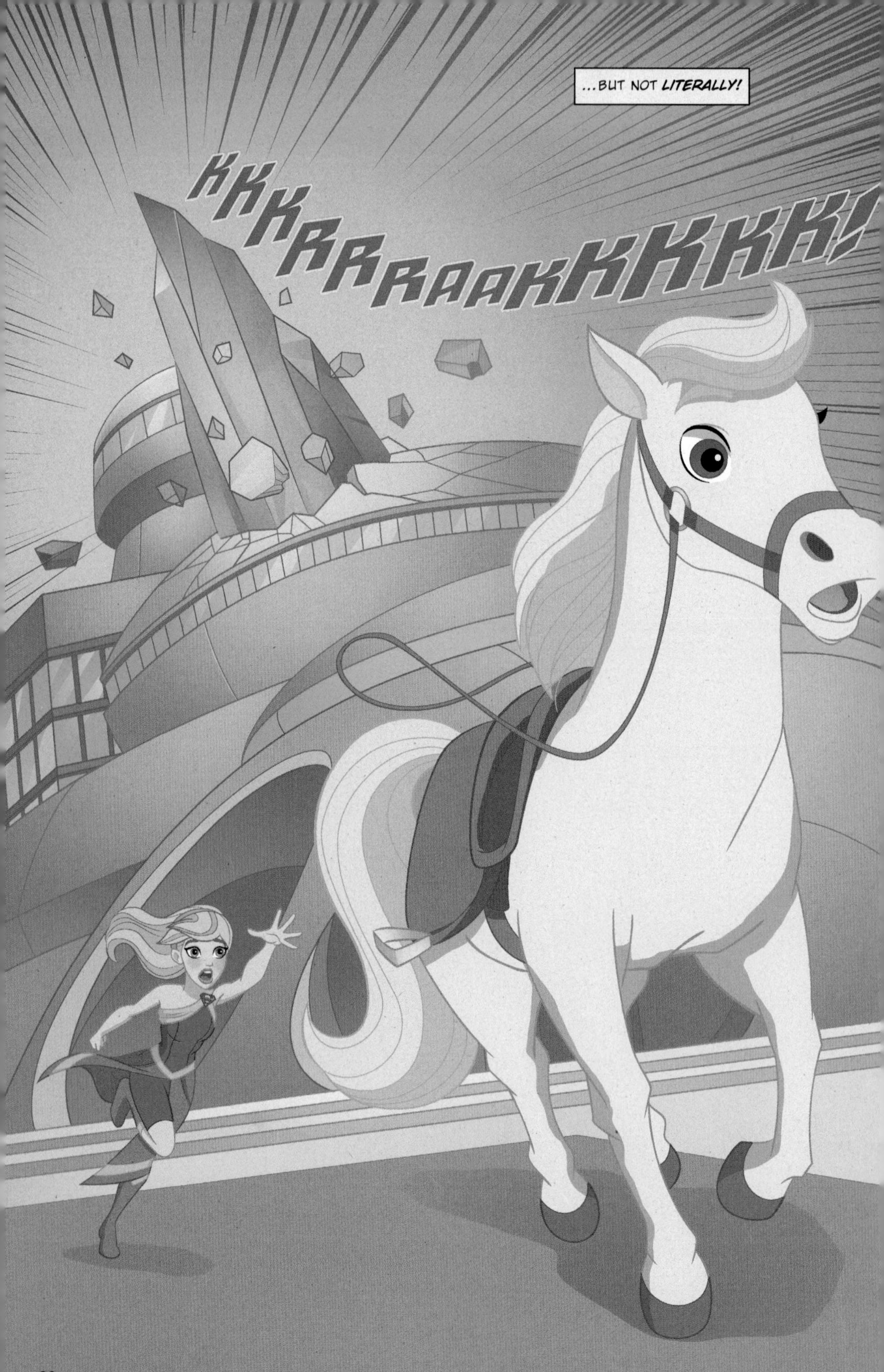
...BUT NOT LITERALLY!
KKKRRRRAAKKKKK!

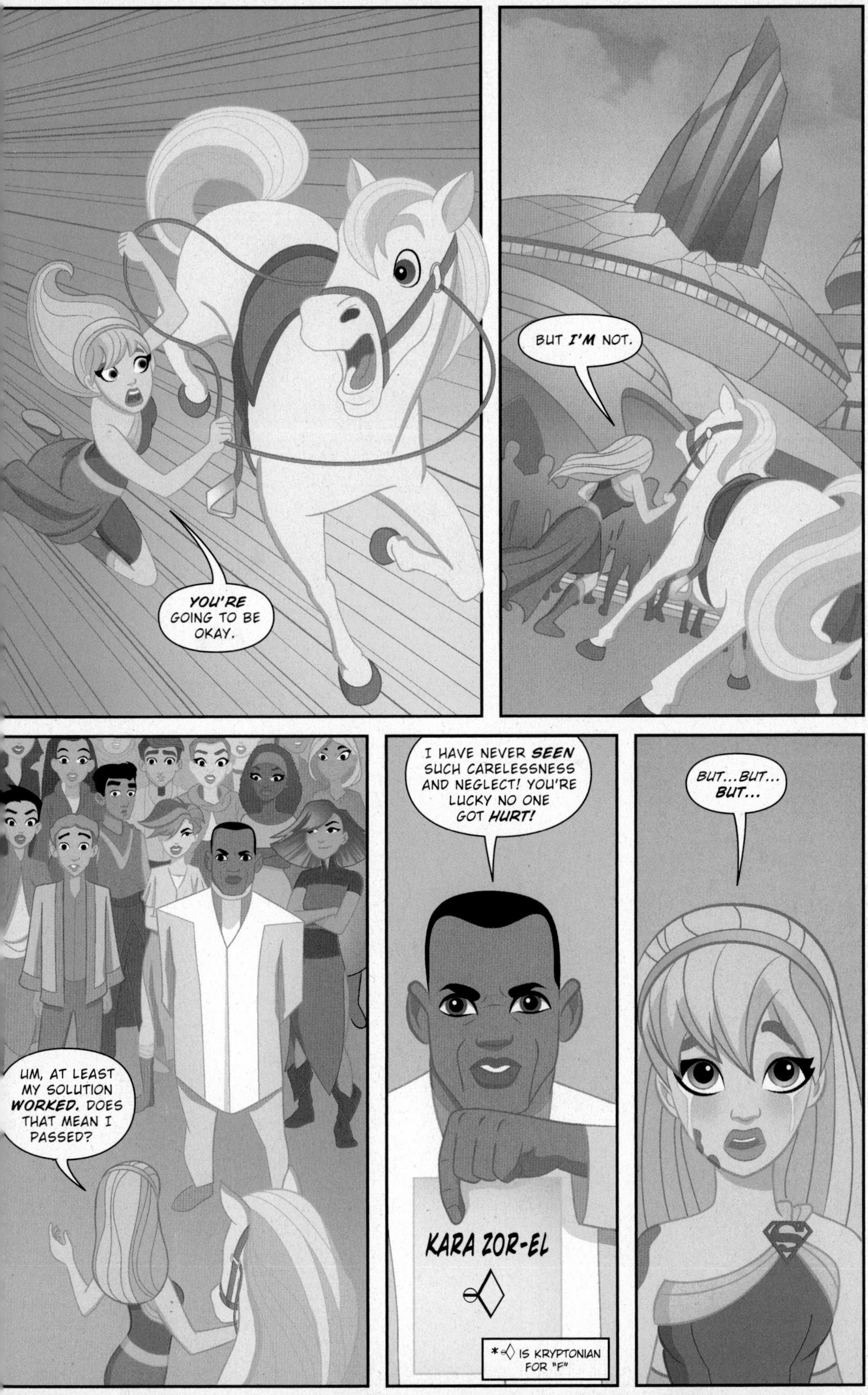
YOU'RE GOING TO BE OKAY.
BUT I'M NOT.
UM, AT LEAST MY SOLUTION WORKED. DOES THAT MEAN I PASSED?
I HAVE NEVER SEEN SUCH CARELESSNESS AND NEGLECT! YOU'RE LUCKY NO ONE GOT HURT!
KARA ZOR-EL
* IS KRYPTONIAN FOR "F"
BUT...BUT... BUT...

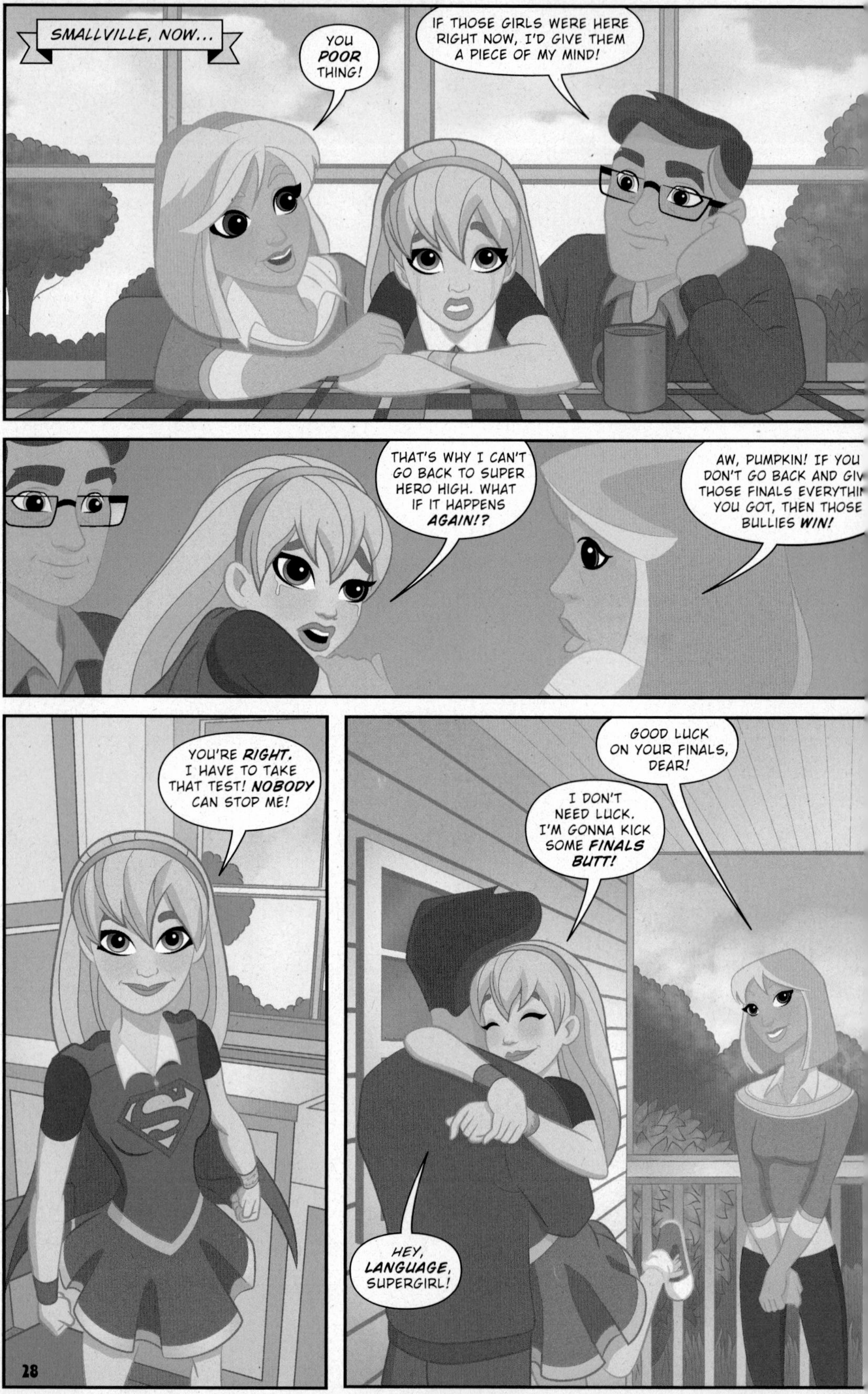
SMALLVILLE, NOW...
YOU POOR THING!
IF THOSE GIRLS WERE HERE RIGHT NOW, I'D GIVE THEM A PIECE OF MY MIND!
THAT'S WHY I CAN'T GO BACK TO SUPER HERO HIGH. WHAT IF IT HAPPENS AGAIN!?
AW, PUMPKIN! IF YOU DON'T GO BACK AND GIV THOSE FINALS EVERYTHI YOU GOT, THEN THOSE BULLIES WIN!
YOU'RE RIGHT. I HAVE TO TAKE THAT TEST! NOBODY CAN STOP ME!
GOOD LUCK ON YOUR FINALS, DEAR!
I DON'T NEED LUCK. I'M GONNA KICK SOME FINALS BUTT!
HEY, LANGUAGE, SUPERGIRL!

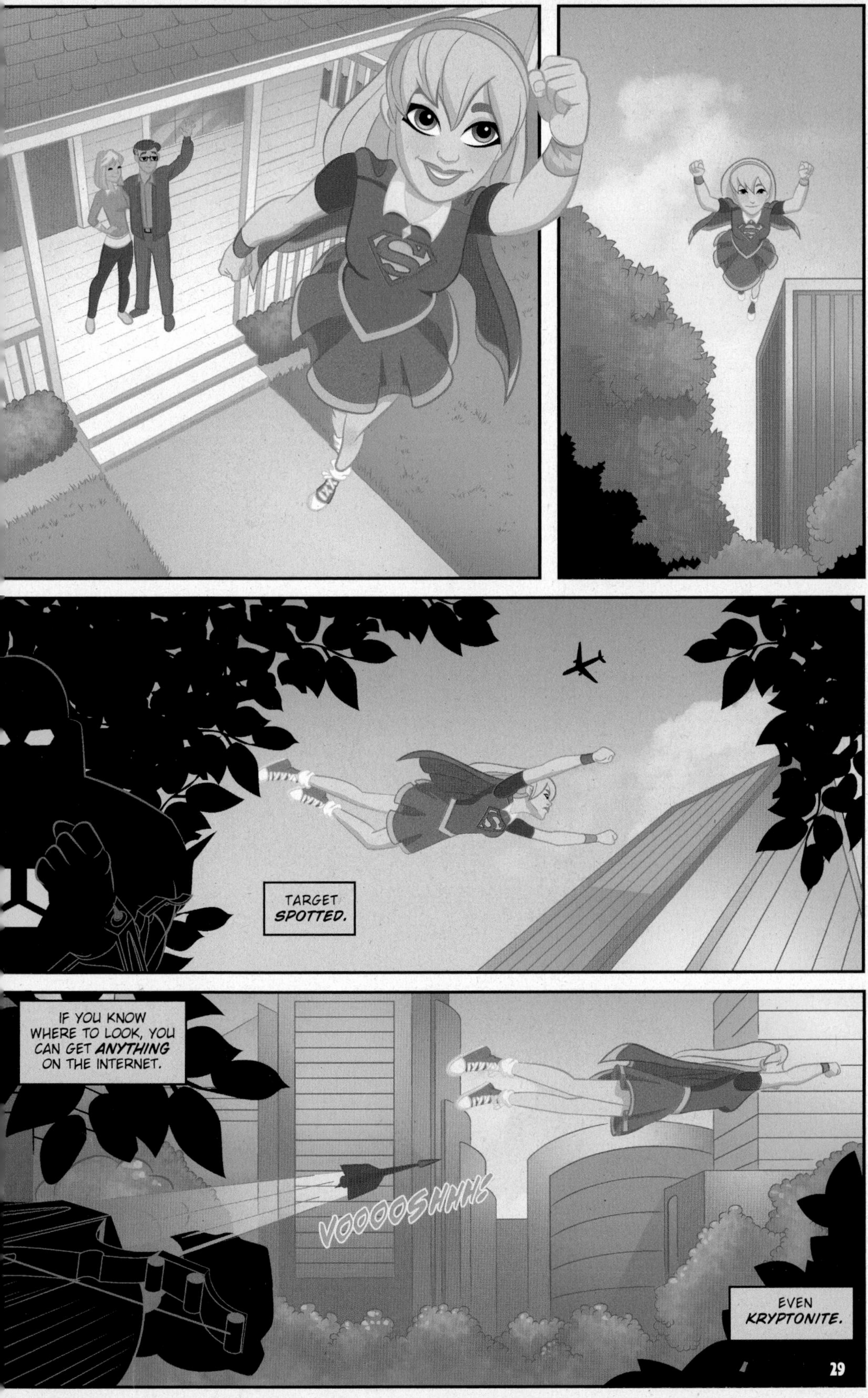
TARGET SPOTTED.
IF YOU KNOW WHERE TO LOOK, YOU CAN GET ANYTHING ON THE INTERNET.
VOOOOSHHHH!
EVEN KRYPTONITE.

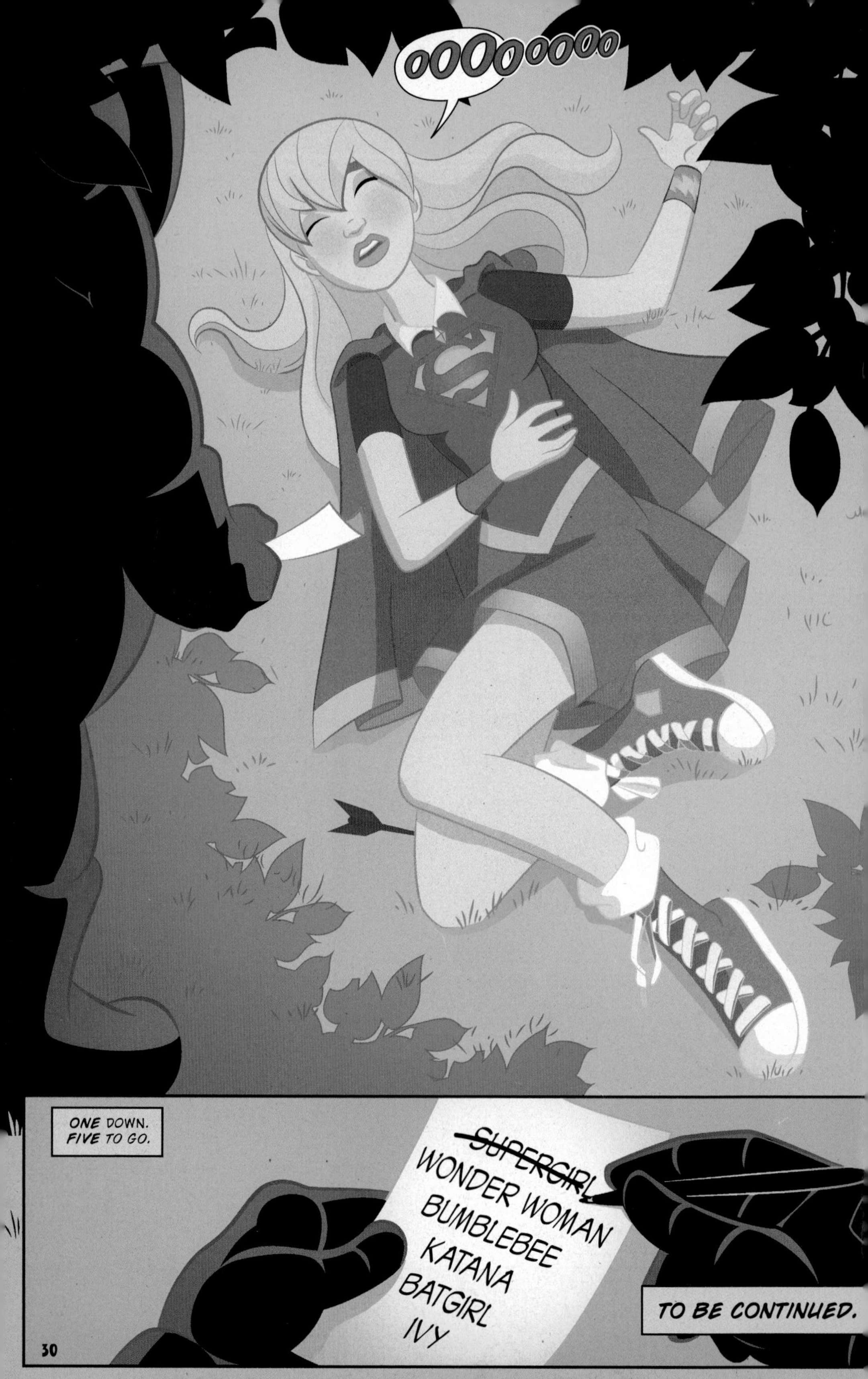
OOOOOOOOO
ONE DOWN. FIVE TO GO.
SUPERGIRL
WONDER WOMAN
BUMBLEBEE
KATANA
BATGIRL
IVY
TO BE CONTINUED.

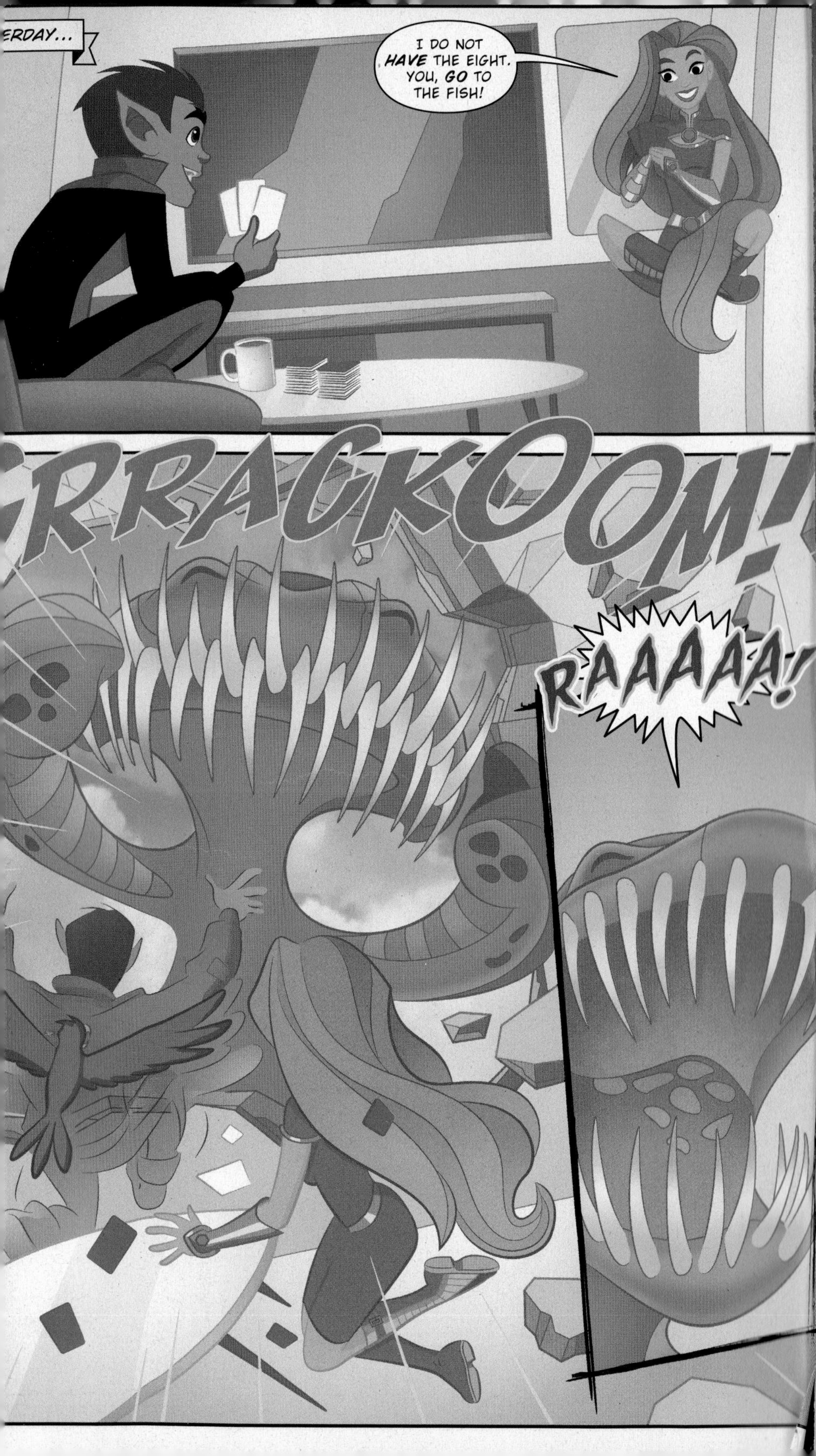
ERDAY...
I DO NOT *HAVE* THE EIGHT. YOU, *GO* TO THE FISH!
RRACKOOM!
RAAAAA!

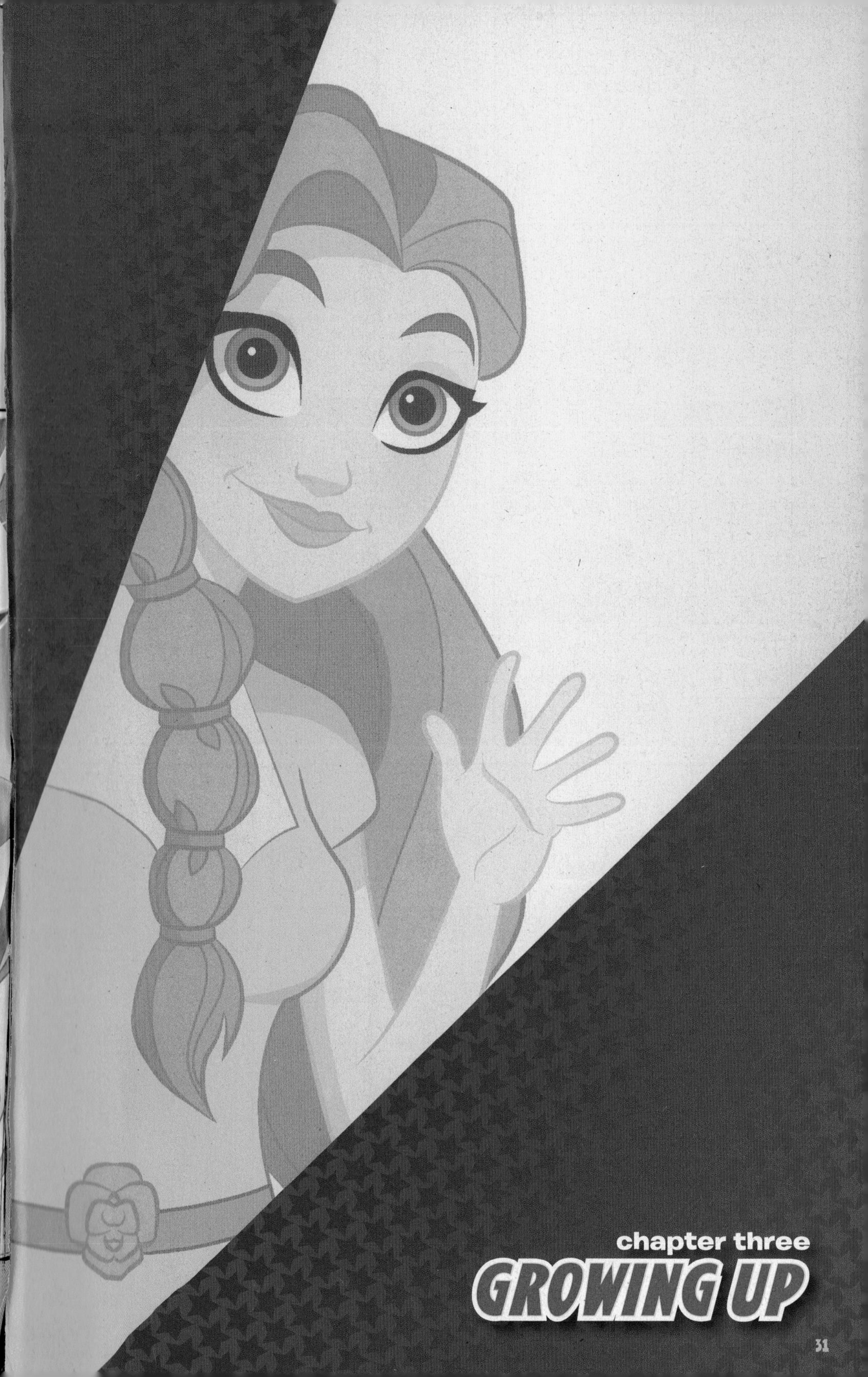

chapter three
GROWING UP

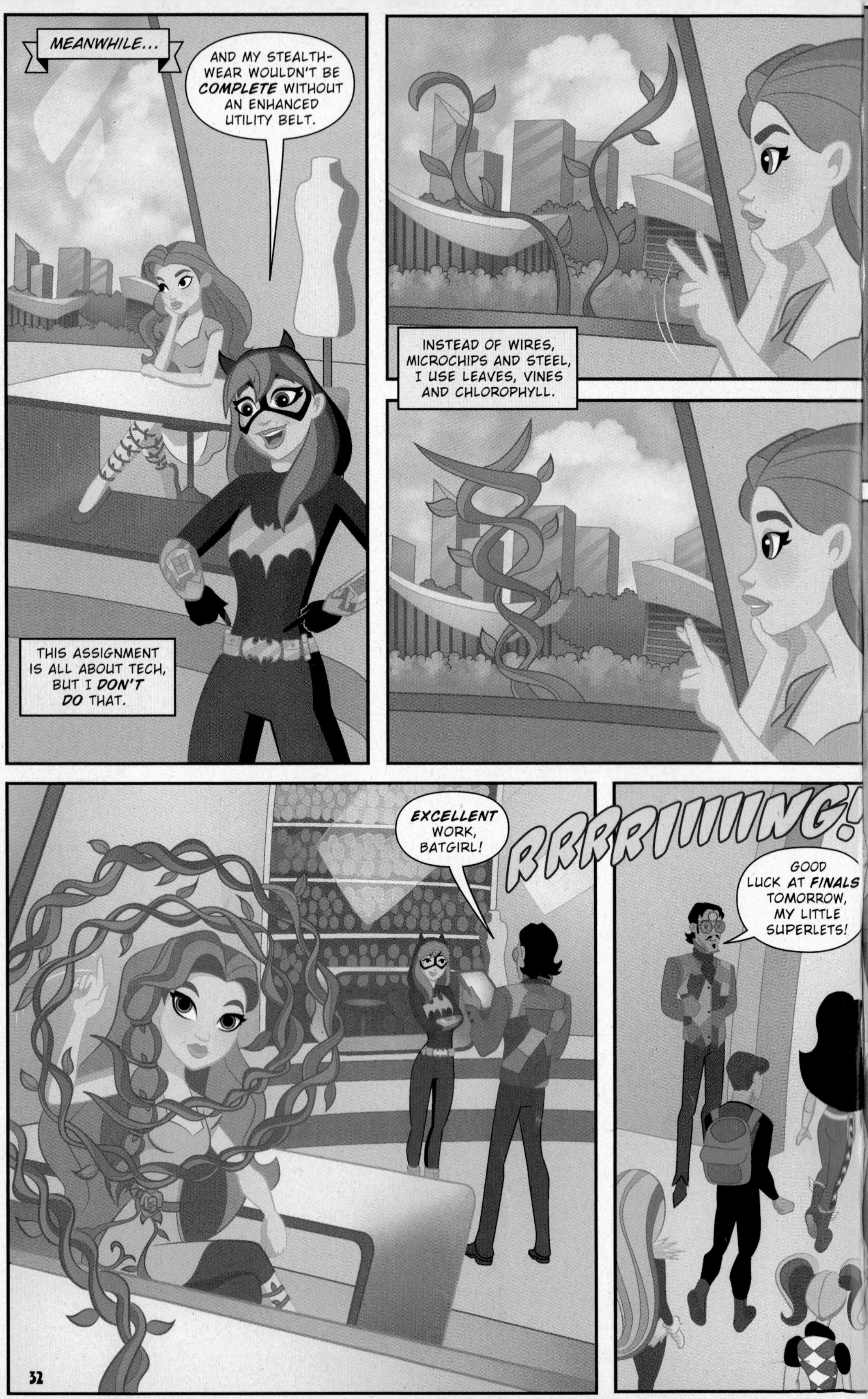
MEANWHILE...
AND MY STEALTH-WEAR WOULDN'T BE *COMPLETE* WITHOUT AN ENHANCED UTILITY BELT.
THIS ASSIGNMENT IS ALL ABOUT TECH, BUT I *DON'T DO* THAT.
INSTEAD OF WIRES, MICROCHIPS AND STEEL, I USE LEAVES, VINES AND CHLOROPHYLL.
EXCELLENT WORK, BATGIRL!
RRRRIIIIING!
GOOD LUCK AT *FINALS* TOMORROW, MY LITTLE SUPERLETS!

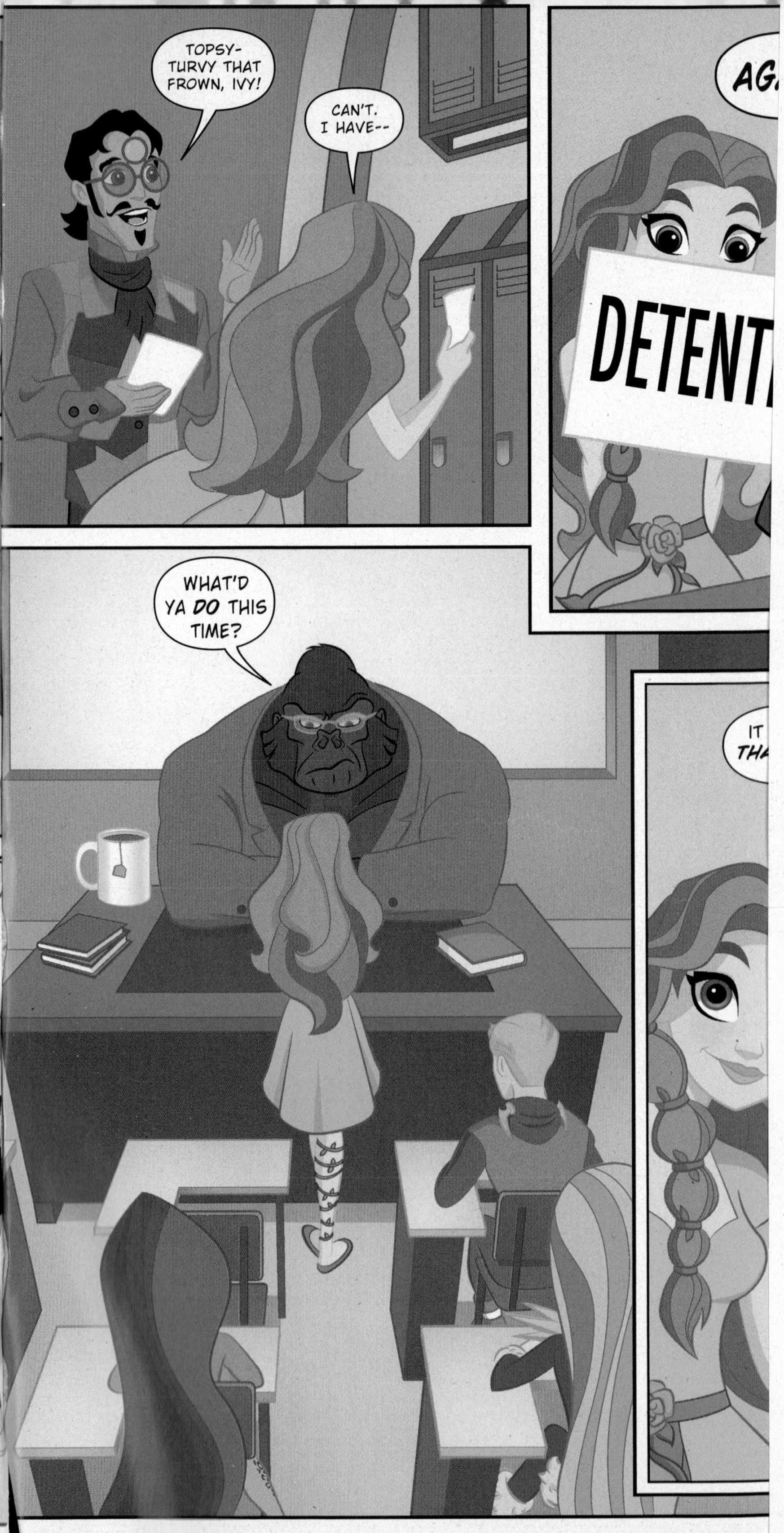
TOPSY-TURVY THAT FROWN, IVY!
CAN'T. I HAVE--
WHAT'D YA *DO* THIS TIME?

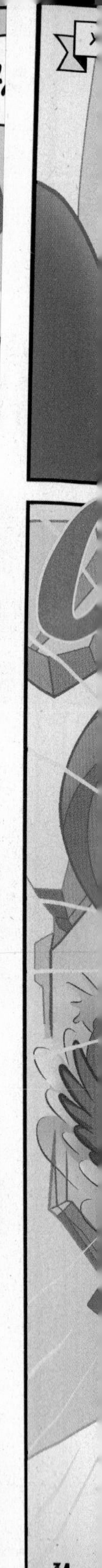

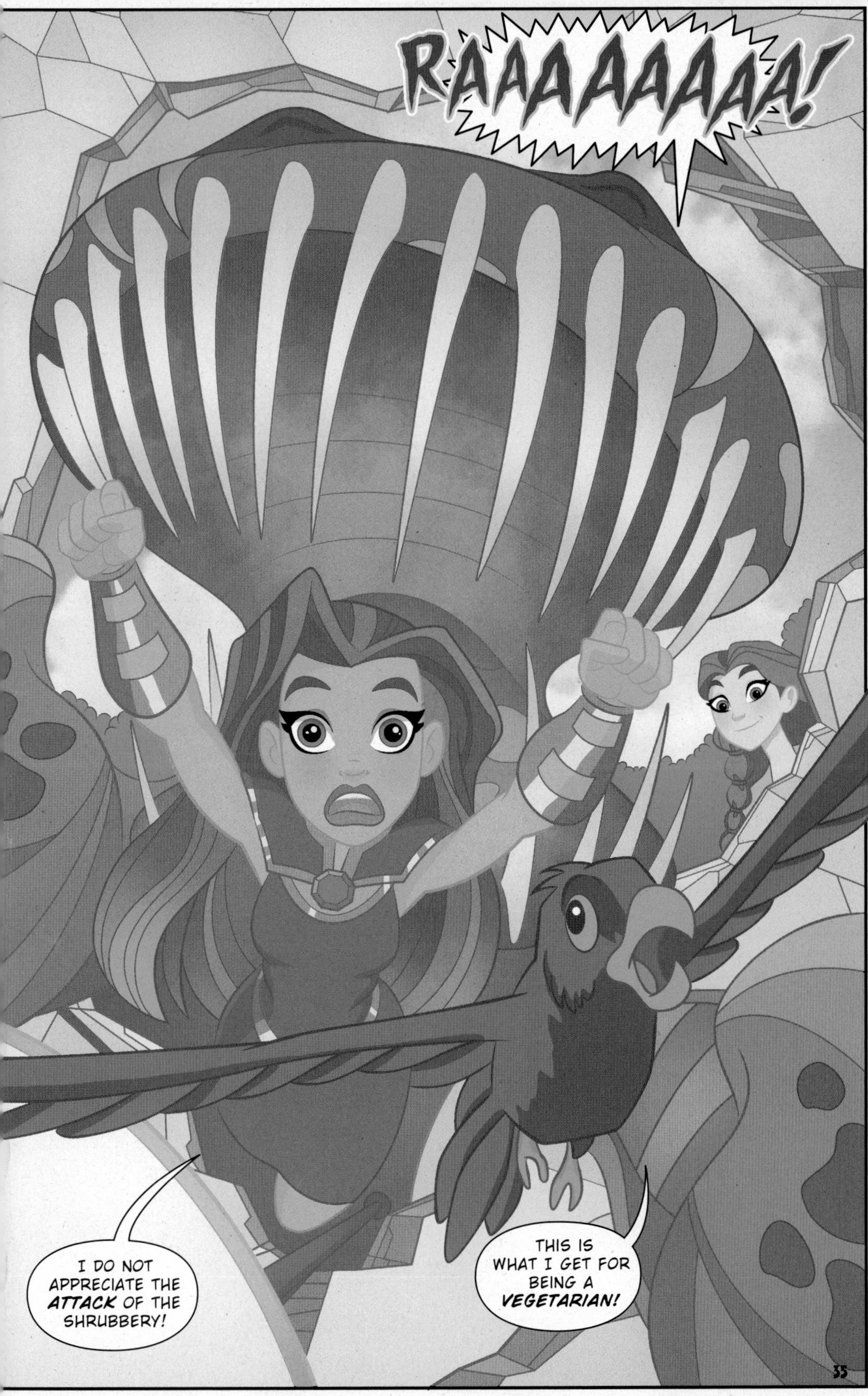
RAAAAAAAA!
I DO NOT APPRECIATE THE ATTACK OF THE SHRUBBERY!
THIS IS WHAT I GET FOR BEING A VEGETARIAN!

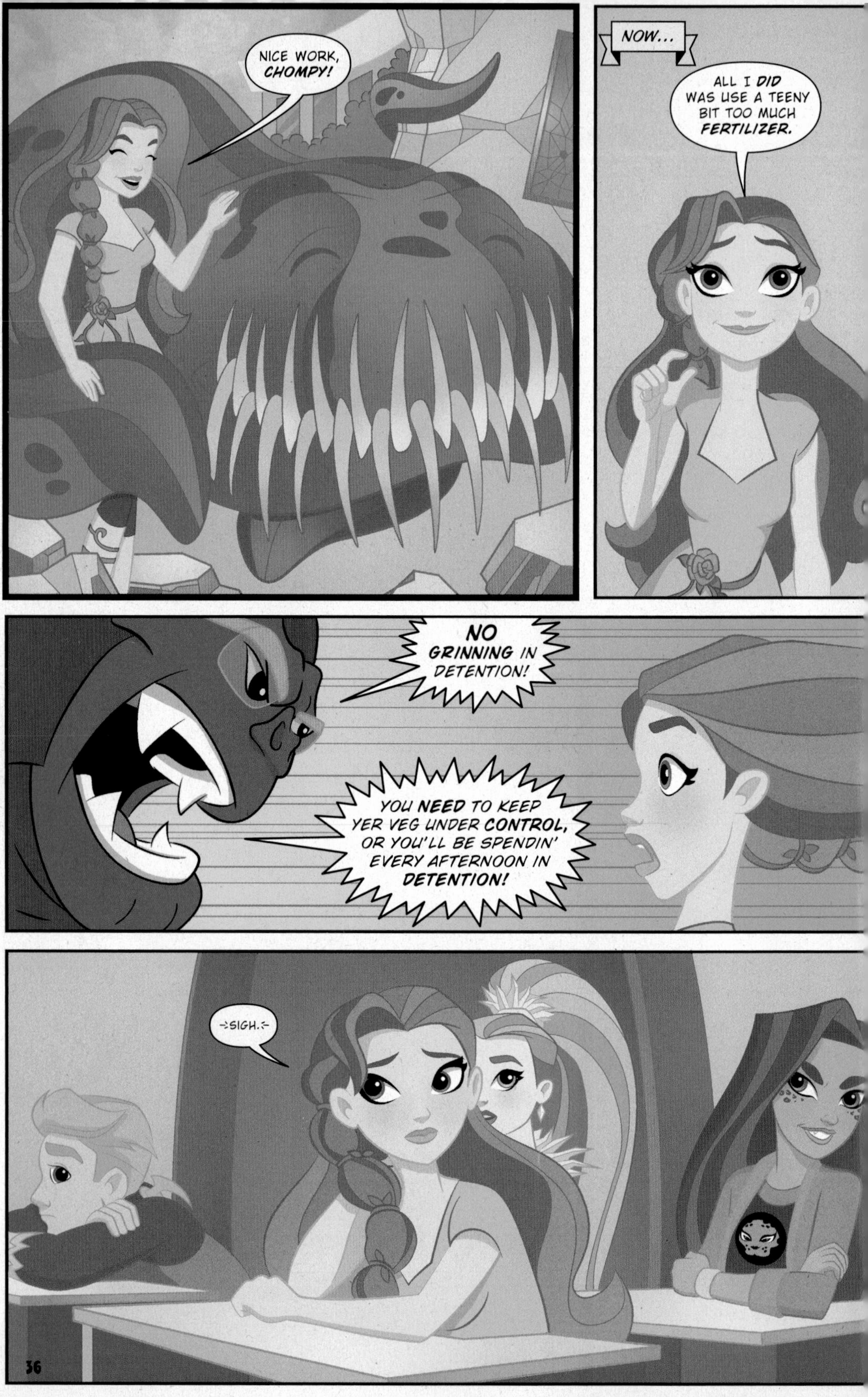
NICE WORK, CHOMPY!
NOW...
ALL I DID WAS USE A TEENY BIT TOO MUCH FERTILIZER.
NO GRINNING IN DETENTION!
YOU NEED TO KEEP YER VEG UNDER CONTROL, OR YOU'LL BE SPENDIN' EVERY AFTERNOON IN DETENTION!
-SIGH.-

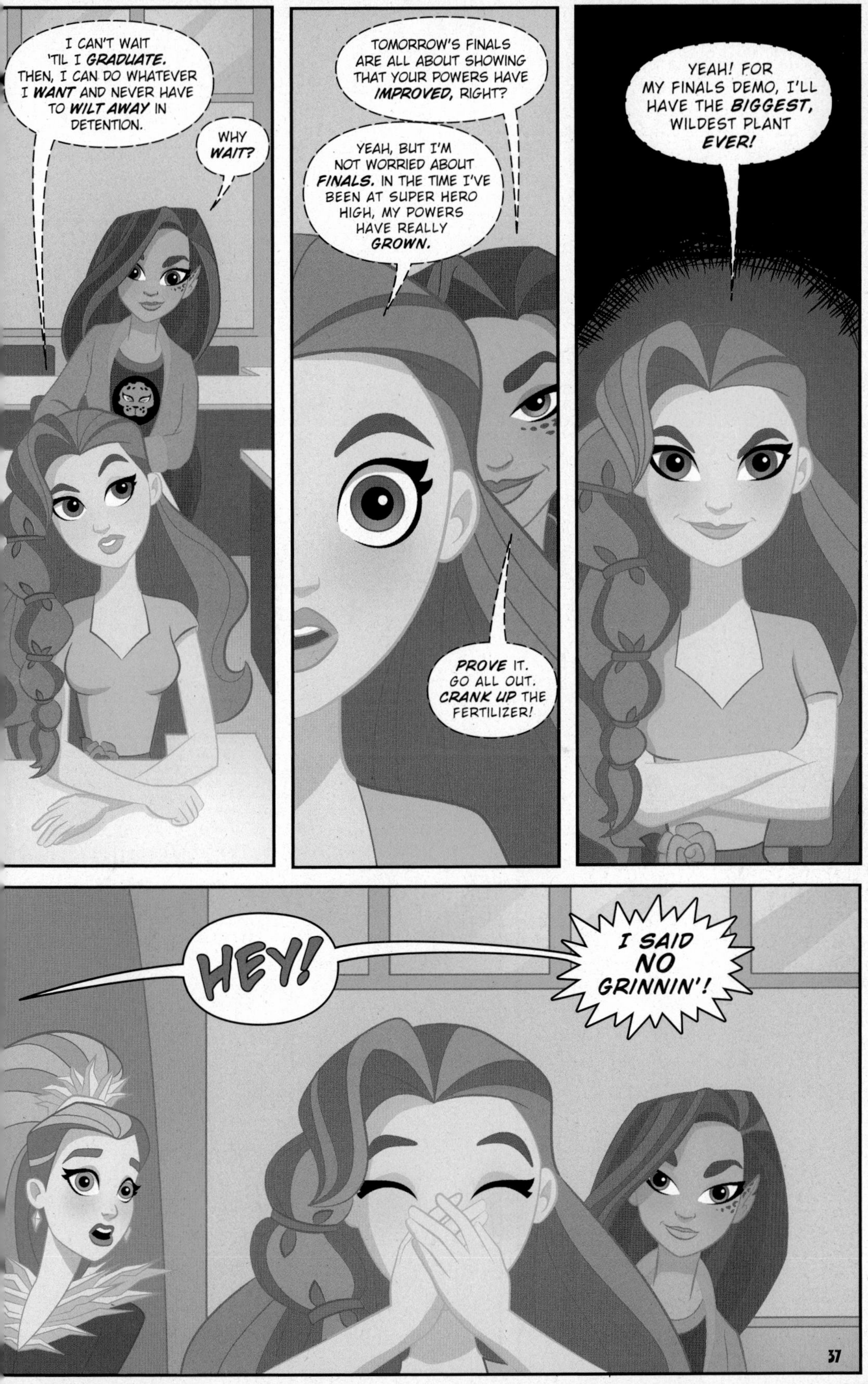
I CAN'T WAIT 'TIL I GRADUATE. THEN, I CAN DO WHATEVER I WANT AND NEVER HAVE TO WILT AWAY IN DETENTION.
WHY WAIT?
TOMORROW'S FINALS ARE ALL ABOUT SHOWING THAT YOUR POWERS HAVE IMPROVED, RIGHT?
YEAH, BUT I'M NOT WORRIED ABOUT FINALS. IN THE TIME I'VE BEEN AT SUPER HERO HIGH, MY POWERS HAVE REALLY GROWN.
PROVE IT. GO ALL OUT. CRANK UP THE FERTILIZER!
YEAH! FOR MY FINALS DEMO, I'LL HAVE THE BIGGEST, WILDEST PLANT EVER!
HEY!
I SAID NO GRINNIN'!

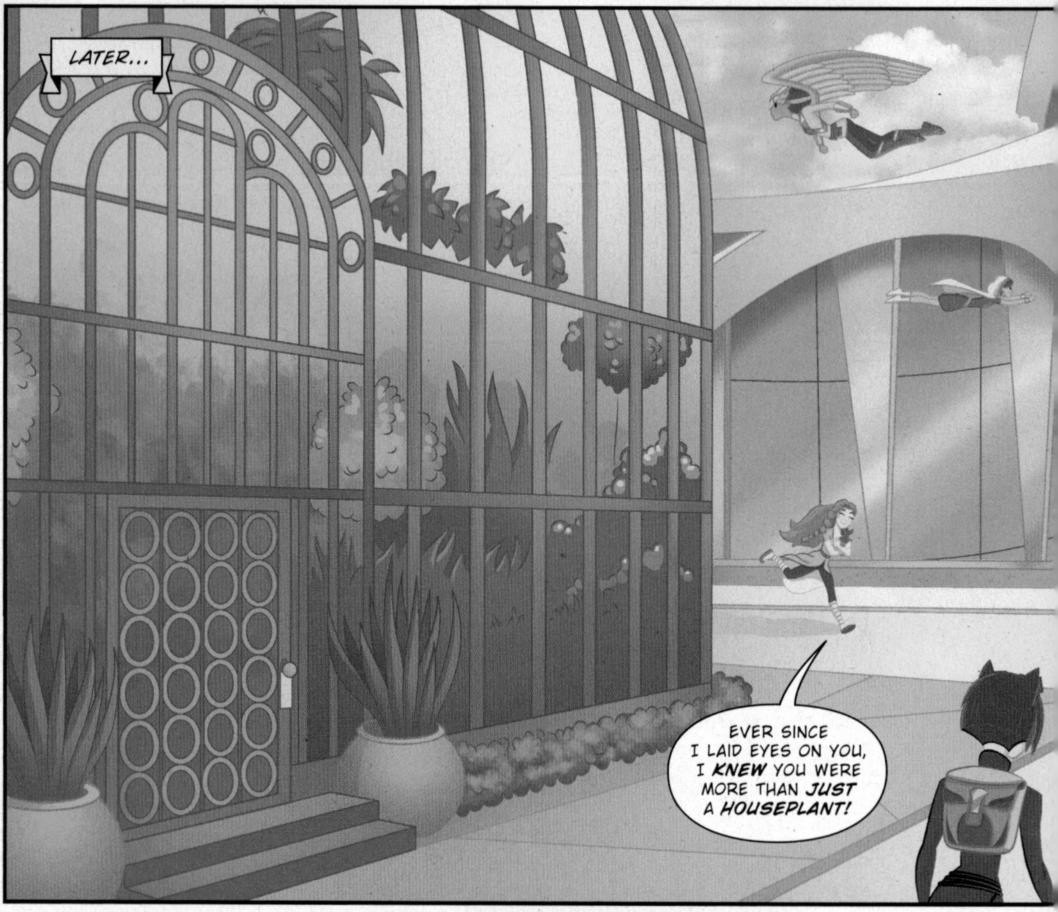
LATER...
EVER SINCE I LAID EYES ON YOU, I KNEW YOU WERE MORE THAN JUST A HOUSEPLANT!

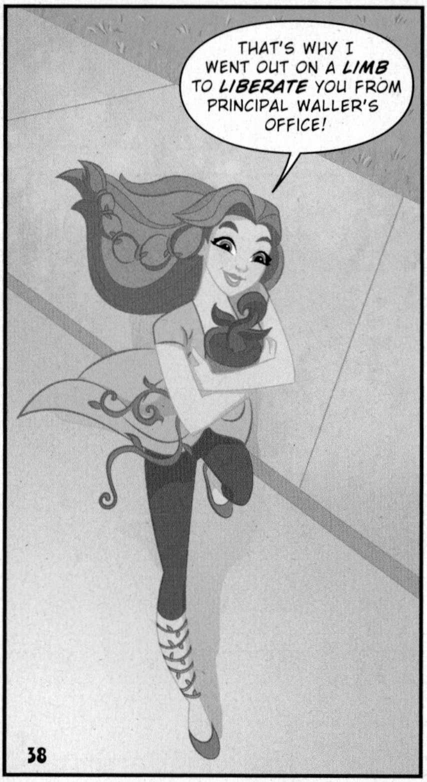
THAT'S WHY I WENT OUT ON A LIMB TO LIBERATE YOU FROM PRINCIPAL WALLER'S OFFICE!

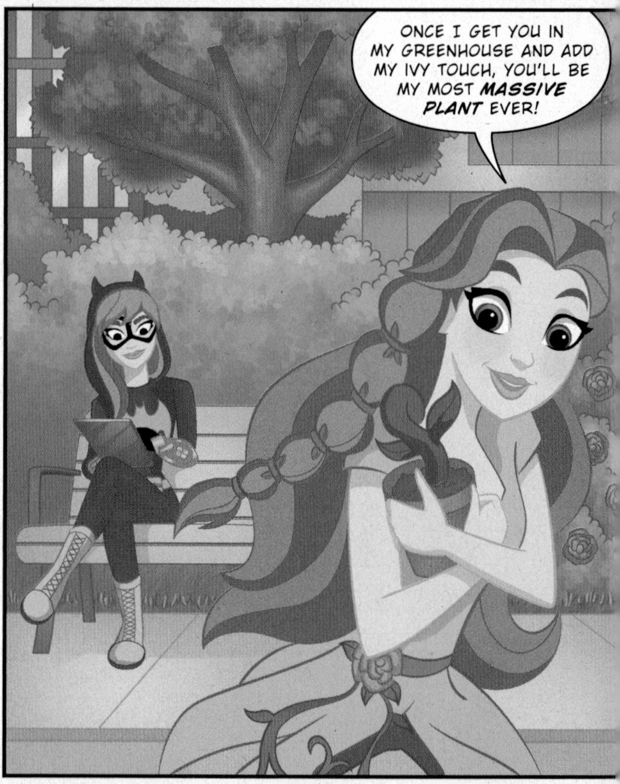
ONCE I GET YOU IN MY GREENHOUSE AND ADD MY IVY TOUCH, YOU'LL BE MY MOST MASSIVE PLANT EVER!

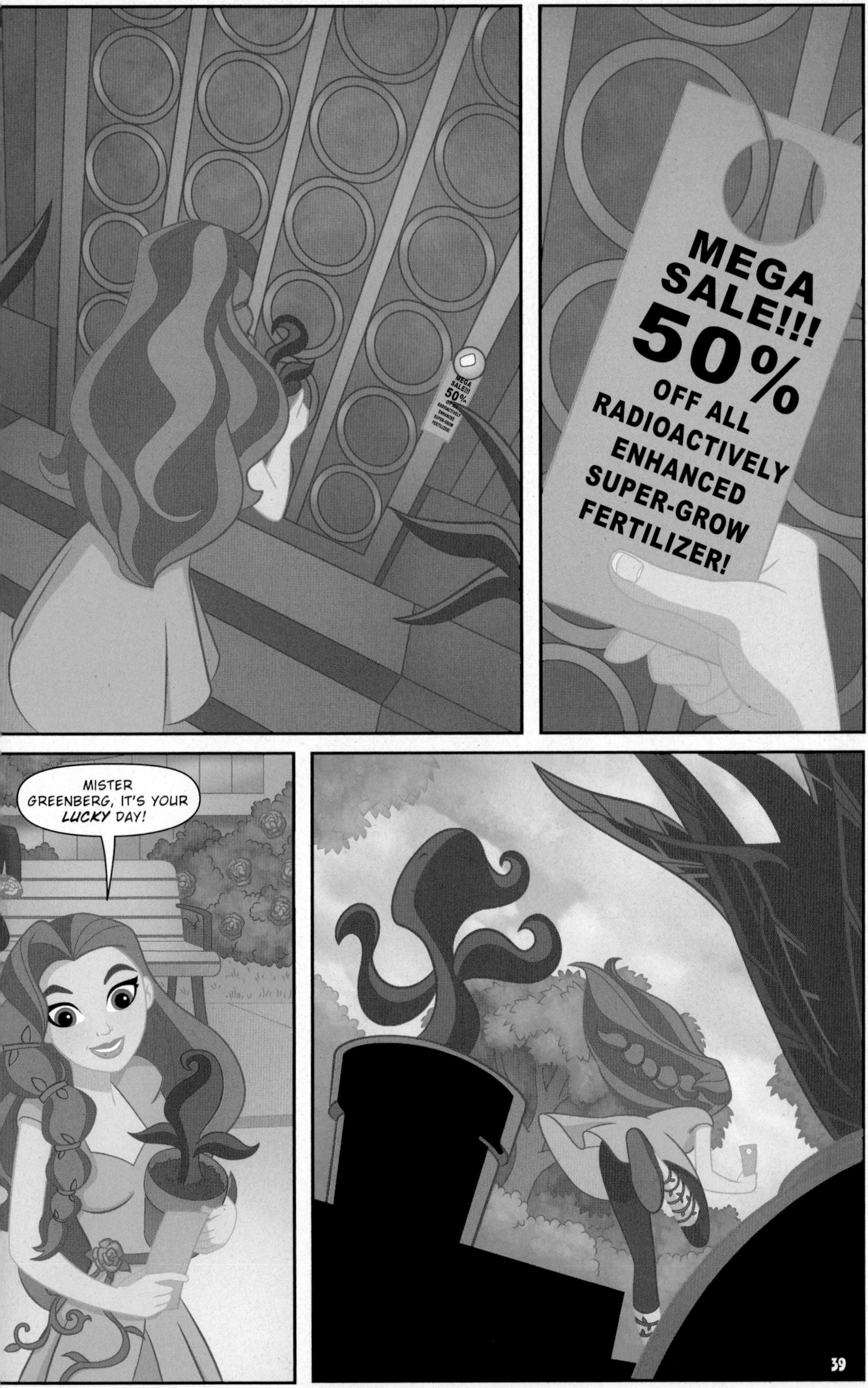
MEGA SALE!!! 50% OFF ALL RADIOACTIVELY ENHANCED SUPER-GROW FERTILIZER!
MEGA SALE!!! 50% OFF ALL RADIOACTIVELY ENHANCED SUPER-GROW FERTILIZER!
MISTER GREENBERG, IT'S YOUR *LUCKY* DAY!

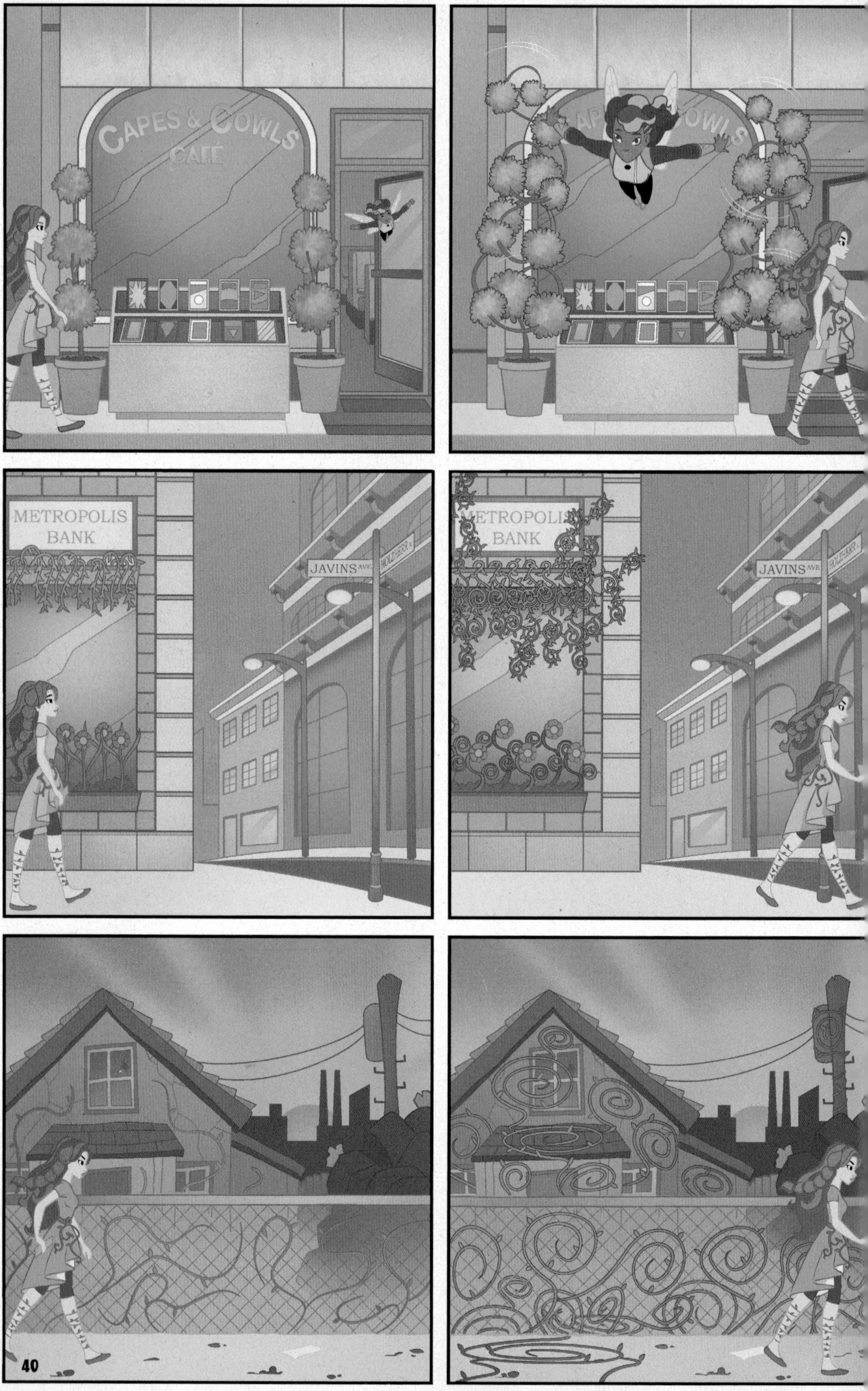
CAPES & COWLS CAFÉ
METROPOLIS BANK
JAVINS AVE

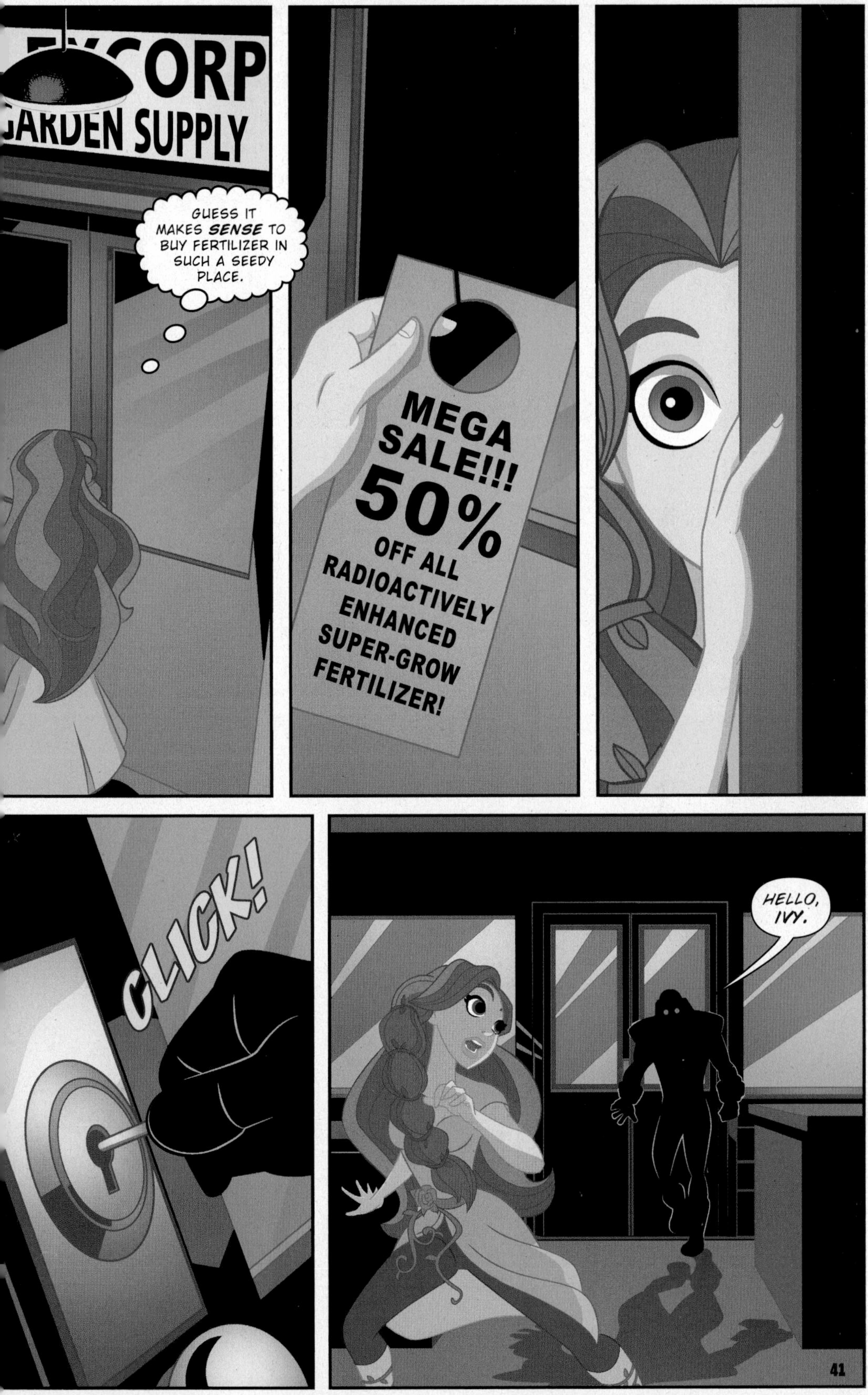

GARDEN SUPPLY
GUESS IT MAKES SENSE TO BUY FERTILIZER IN SUCH A SEEDY PLACE.
MEGA SALE!!! 50% OFF ALL RADIOACTIVELY ENHANCED SUPER-GROW FERTILIZER!
CLICK!
HELLO, IVY.

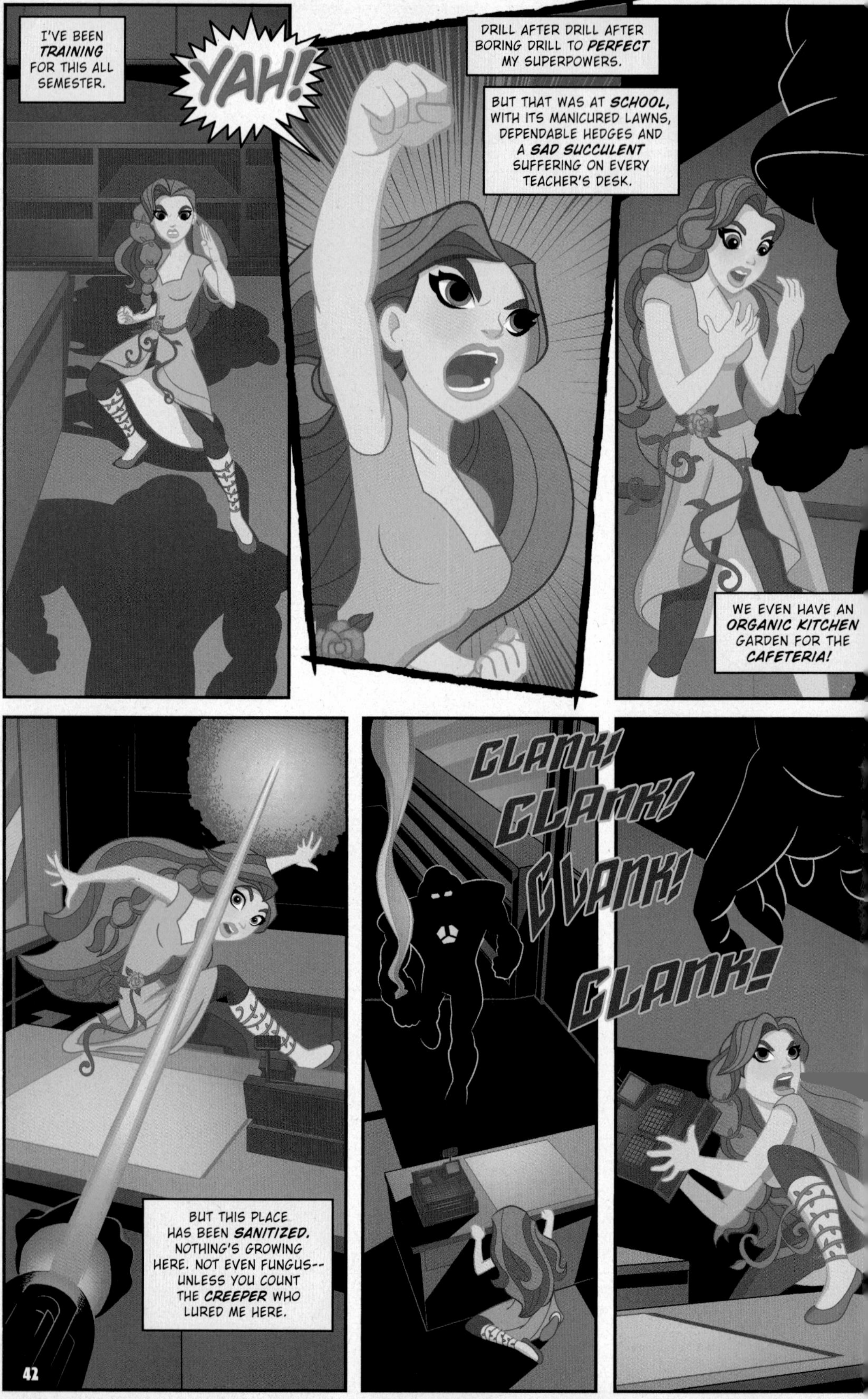

I'VE BEEN TRAINING FOR THIS ALL SEMESTER.
YAH!
DRILL AFTER DRILL AFTER BORING DRILL TO PERFECT MY SUPERPOWERS.
BUT THAT WAS AT SCHOOL, WITH ITS MANICURED LAWNS, DEPENDABLE HEDGES AND A SAD SUCCULENT SUFFERING ON EVERY TEACHER'S DESK.
WE EVEN HAVE AN ORGANIC KITCHEN GARDEN FOR THE CAFETERIA!
BUT THIS PLACE HAS BEEN SANITIZED. NOTHING'S GROWING HERE. NOT EVEN FUNGUS-- UNLESS YOU COUNT THE CREEPER WHO LURED ME HERE.
CLANK!
CLANK!
CLANK!
CLANK!

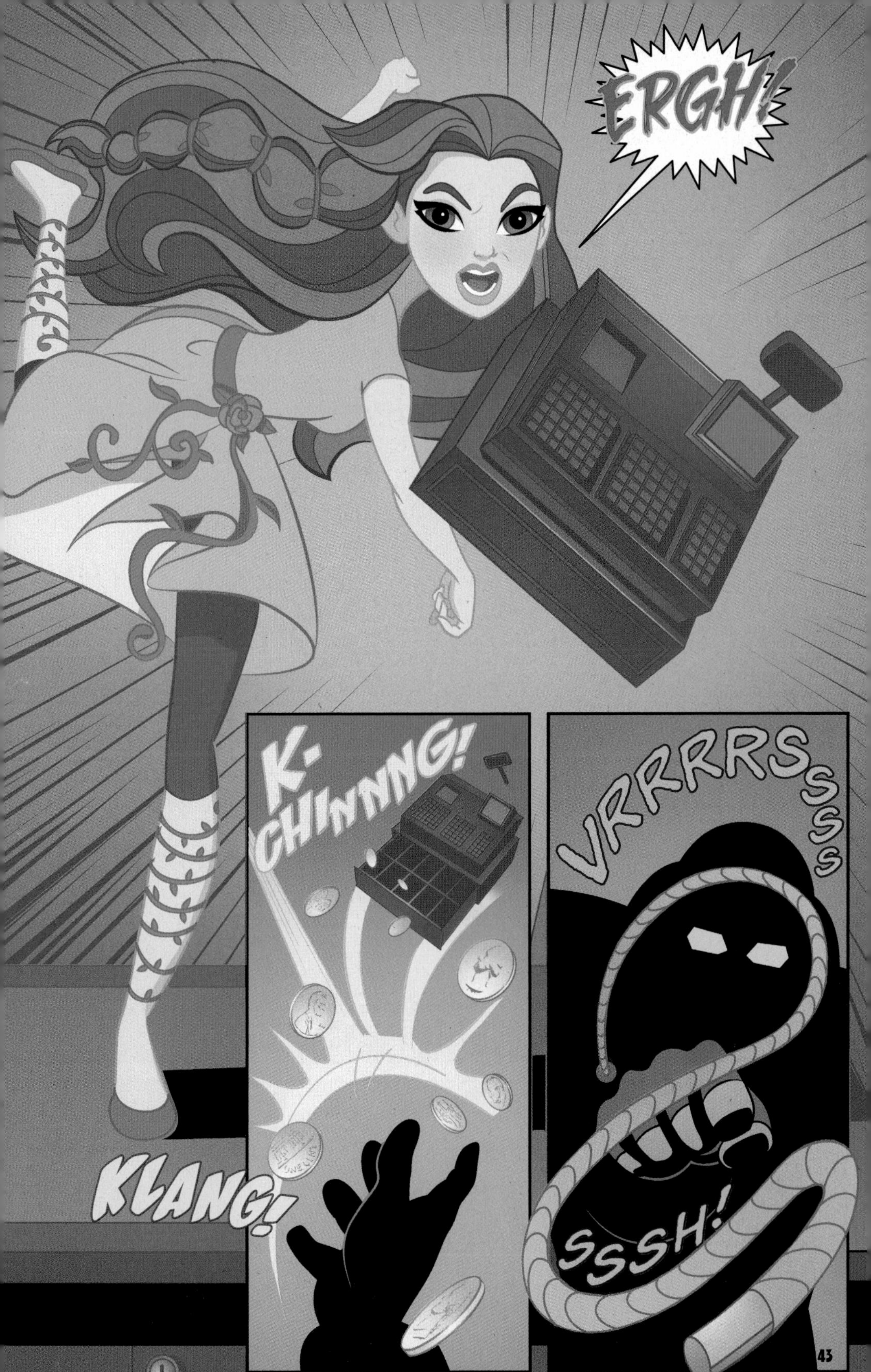
ERGH!
K-CHINNNG!
VRRRRSSSSS
KLANG!
SSSH!

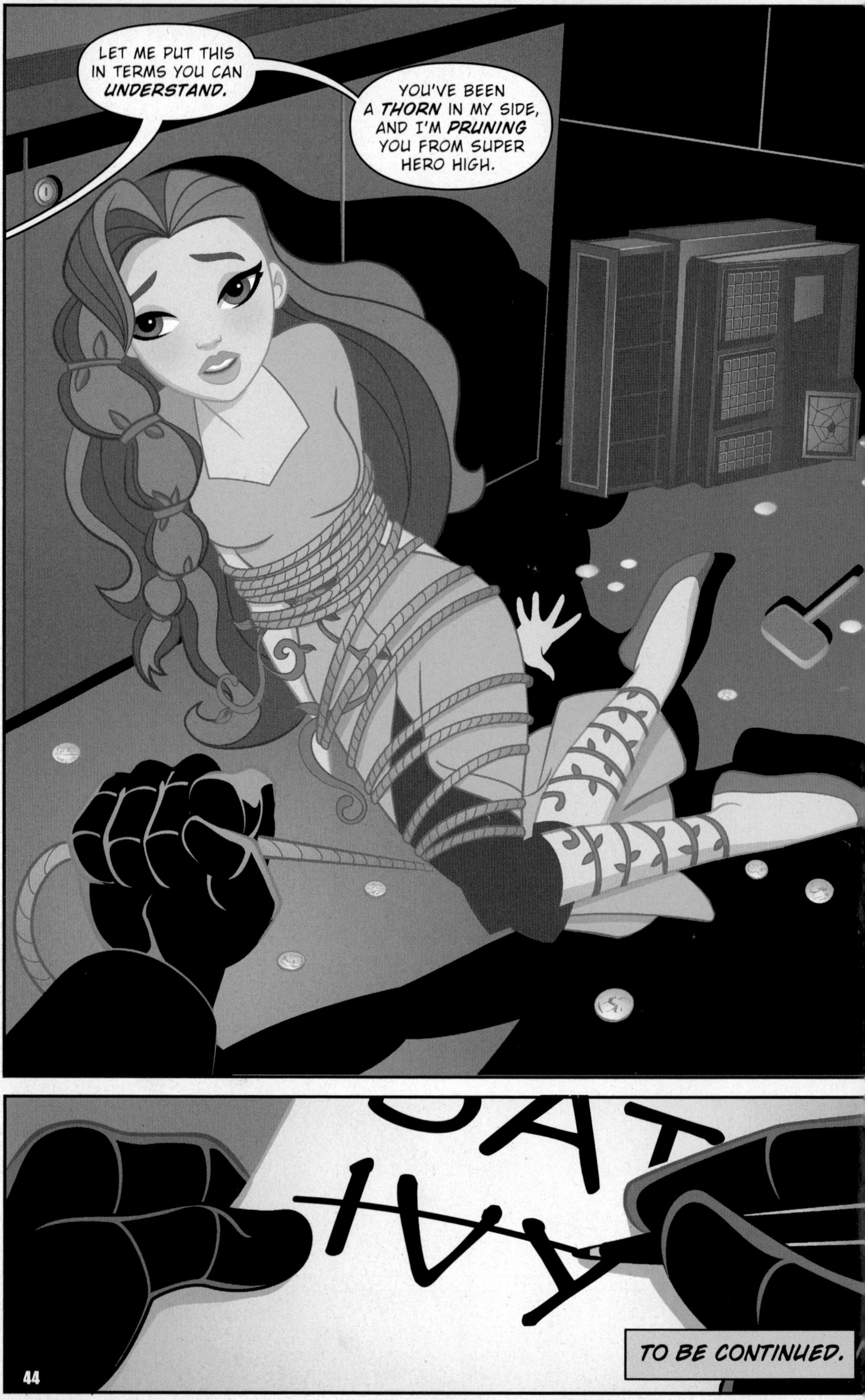
LET ME PUT THIS IN TERMS YOU CAN UNDERSTAND.
YOU'VE BEEN A THORN IN MY SIDE, AND I'M PRUNING YOU FROM SUPER HERO HIGH.
TO BE CONTINUED.

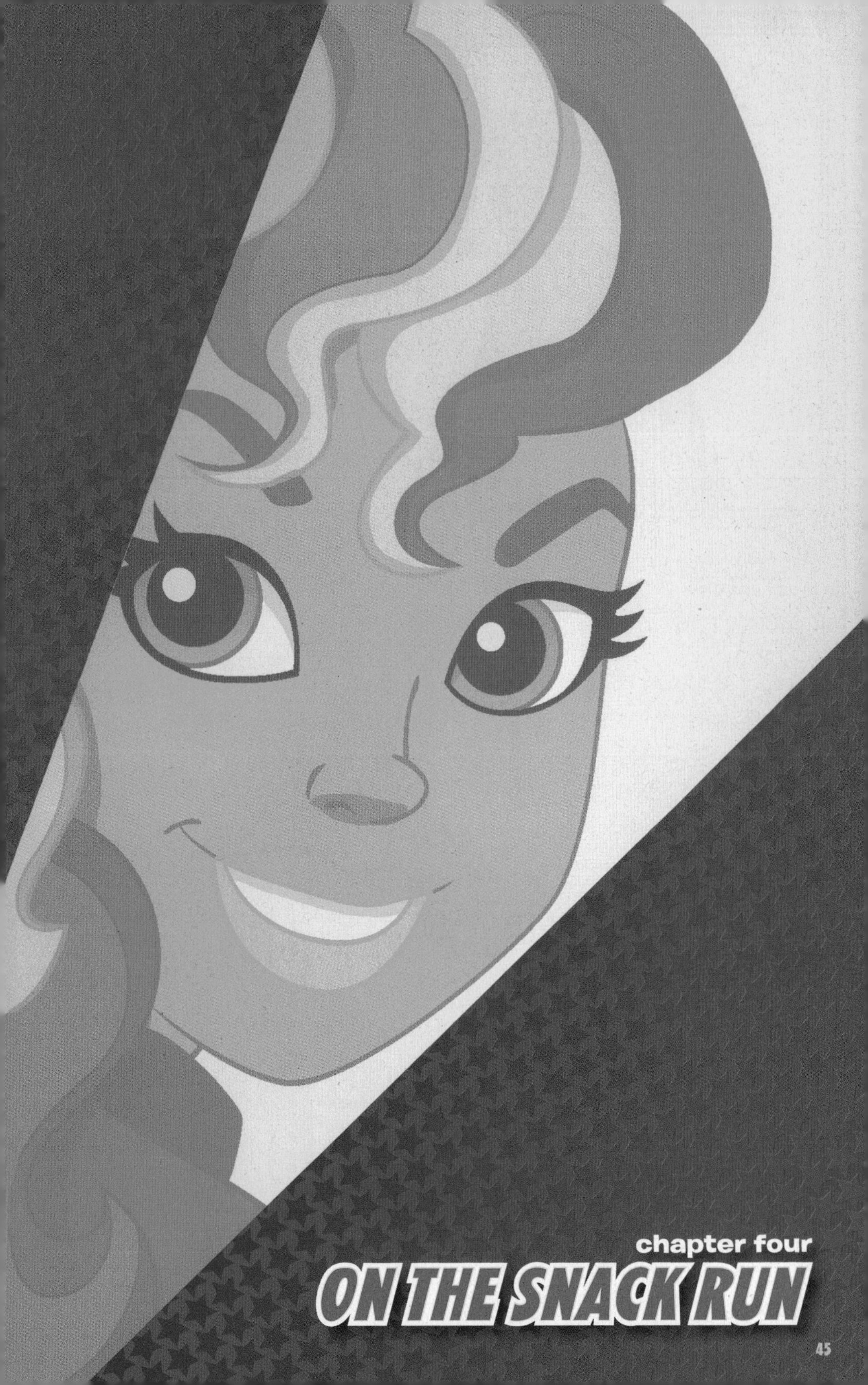

chapter four

ON THE SNACK RUN

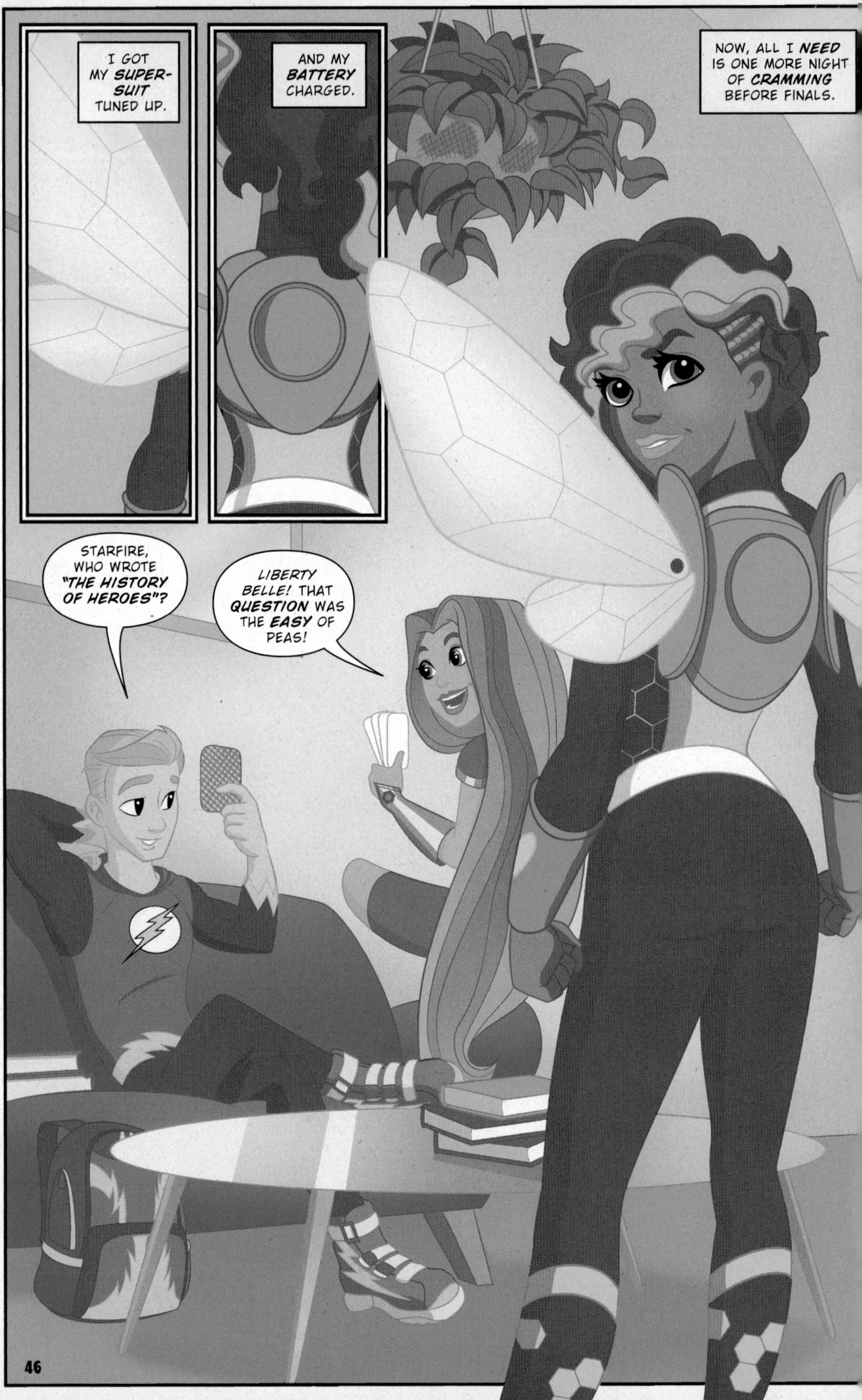
I GOT MY SUPER-SUIT TUNED UP.
AND MY BATTERY CHARGED.
NOW, ALL I NEED IS ONE MORE NIGHT OF CRAMMING BEFORE FINALS.
STARFIRE, WHO WROTE "THE HISTORY OF HEROES"?
LIBERTY BELLE! THAT QUESTION WAS THE EASY OF PEAS!

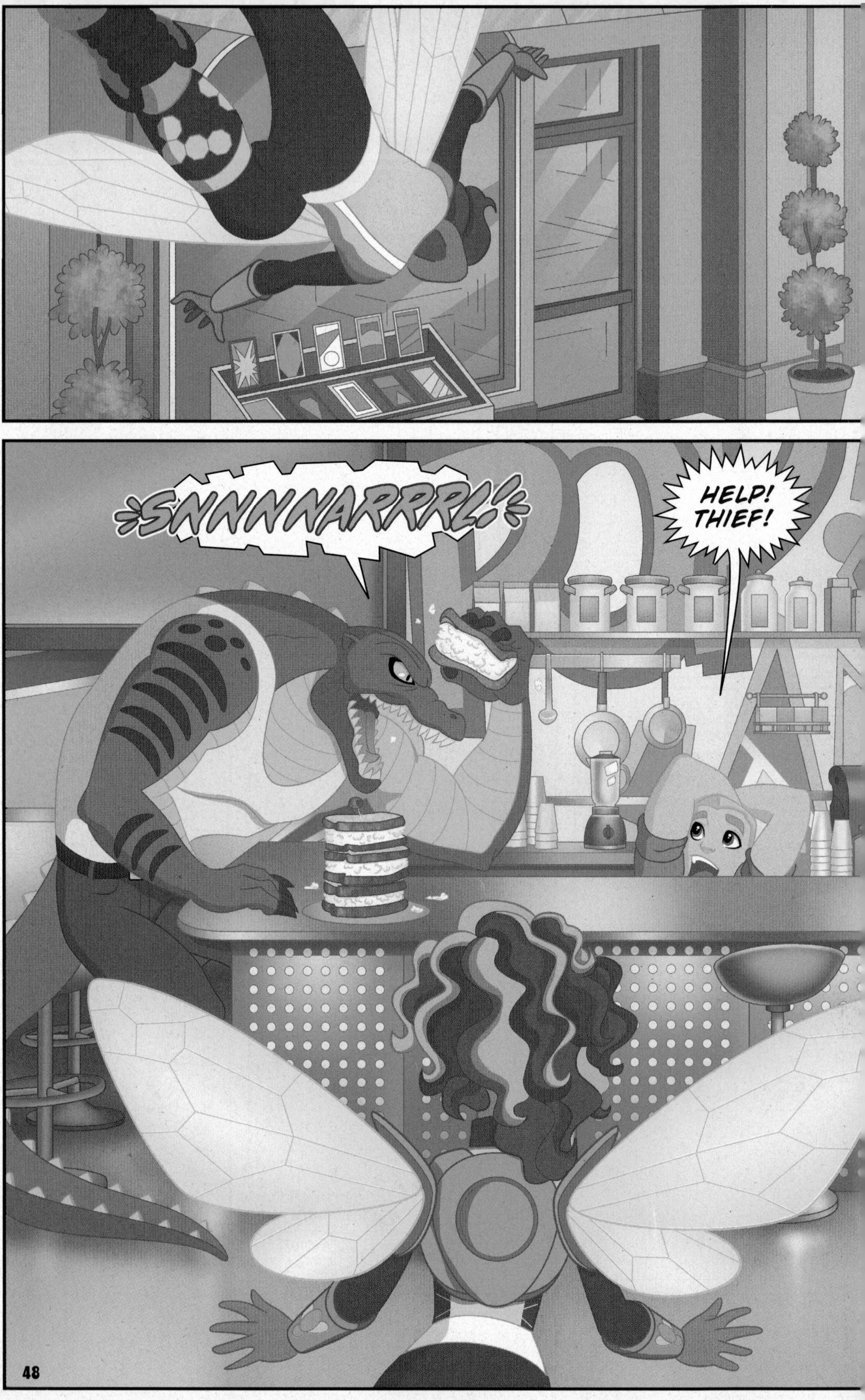
SNNNNARRRL!
HELP! THIEF!

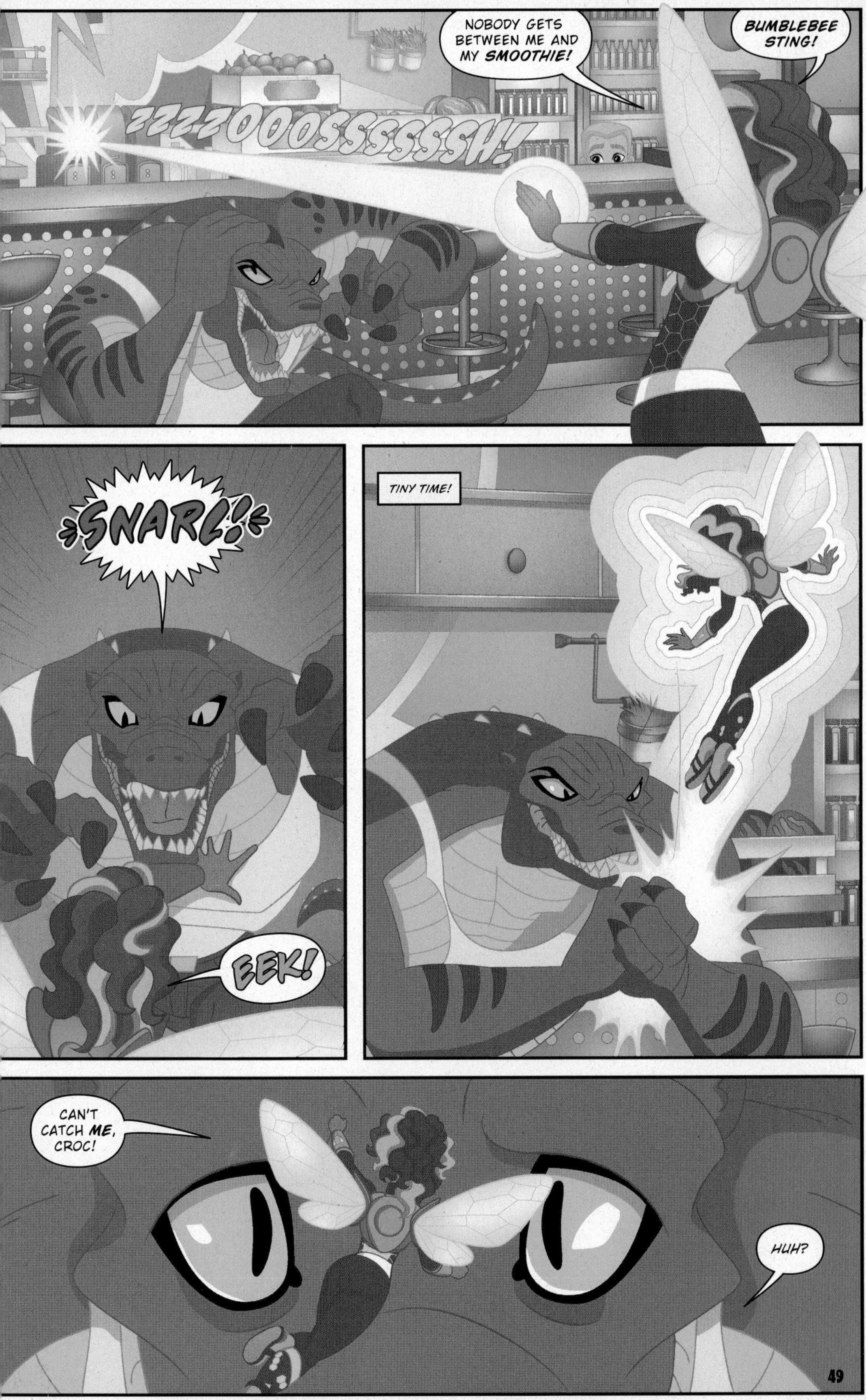
NOBODY GETS BETWEEN ME AND MY SMOOTHIE!
BUMBLEBEE STING!
ZZZZOOOSSSSSSH!
SNARL!
EEK!
TINY TIME!
CAN'T CATCH ME, CROC!
HUH?

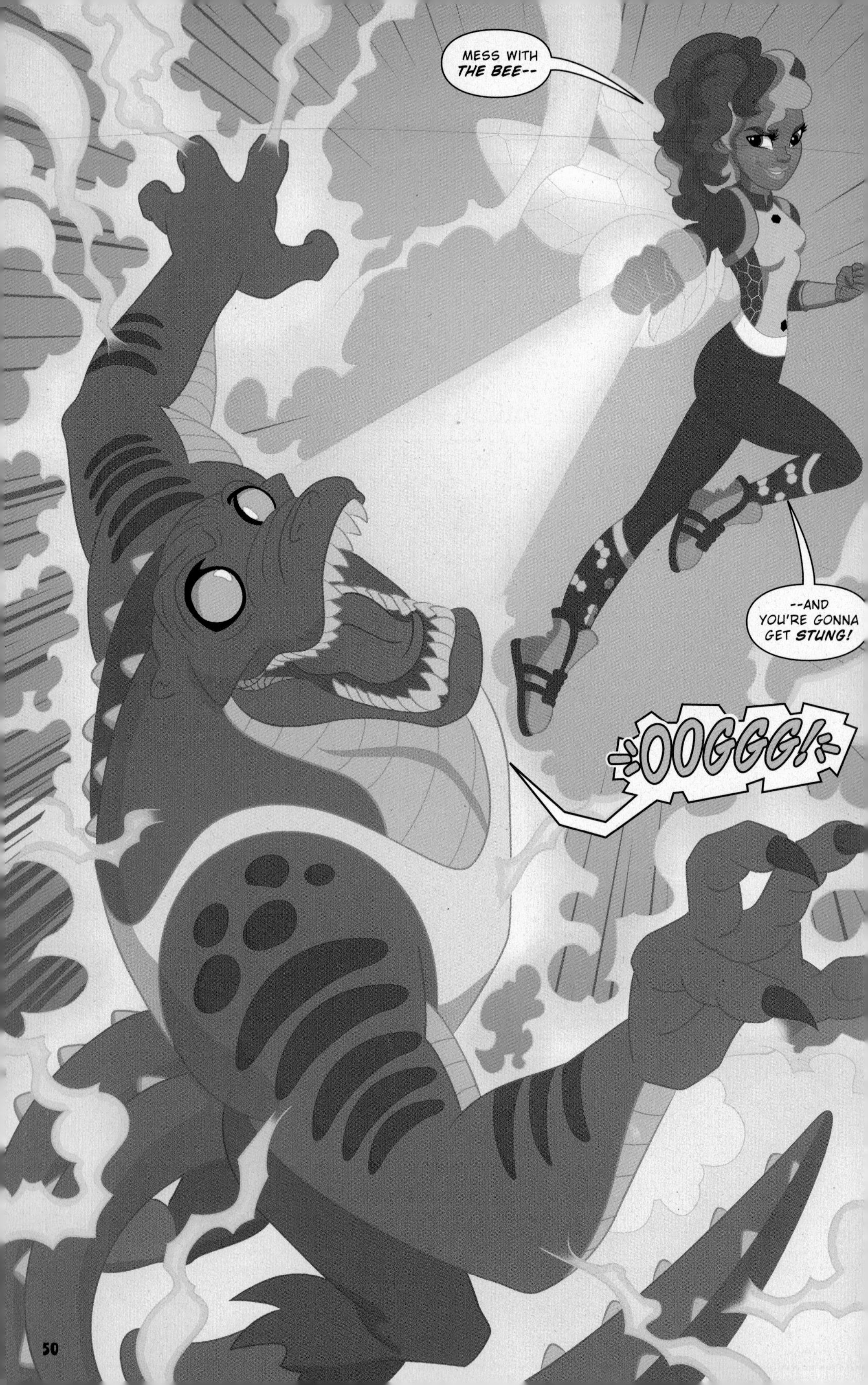
MESS WITH THE BEE--
--AND YOU'RE GONNA GET STUNG!
OOGGG!

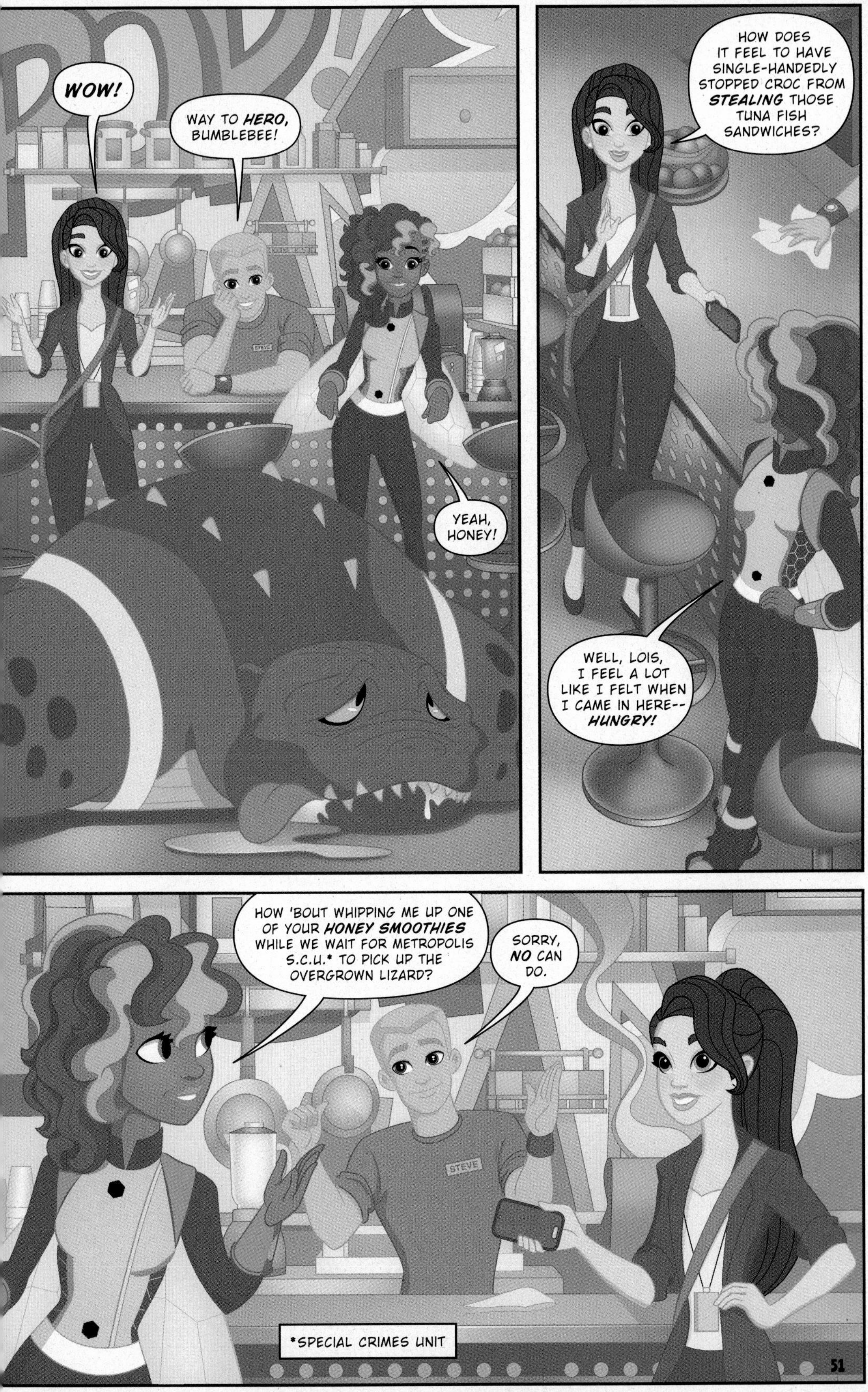
WOW!
WAY TO HERO, BUMBLEBEE!
YEAH, HONEY!
HOW DOES IT FEEL TO HAVE SINGLE-HANDEDLY STOPPED CROC FROM STEALING THOSE TUNA FISH SANDWICHES?
WELL, LOIS, I FEEL A LOT LIKE I FELT WHEN I CAME IN HERE-- HUNGRY!
HOW 'BOUT WHIPPING ME UP ONE OF YOUR HONEY SMOOTHIES WHILE WE WAIT FOR METROPOLIS S.C.U.* TO PICK UP THE OVERGROWN LIZARD?
SORRY, NO CAN DO.
*SPECIAL CRIMES UNIT
STEVE

GUESS YOUR ELECTRIC STINGS ARE AS GOOD AT TAKING OUT SMOOTHIE MACHINES AS THEY ARE AT TAKING OUT VILLAINS.

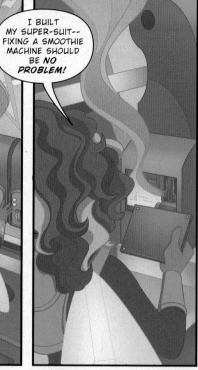

I BUILT MY SUPER-SUIT-- FIXING A SMOOTHIE MACHINE SHOULD BE *NO PROBLEM!*

I JUST NEED TO BORROW A *SOLAR RECONFLABULATOR* FROM THE WEAPONOMICS SUPPLY CLOSET AND I CAN MAKE IT *GOOD AS NEW!*

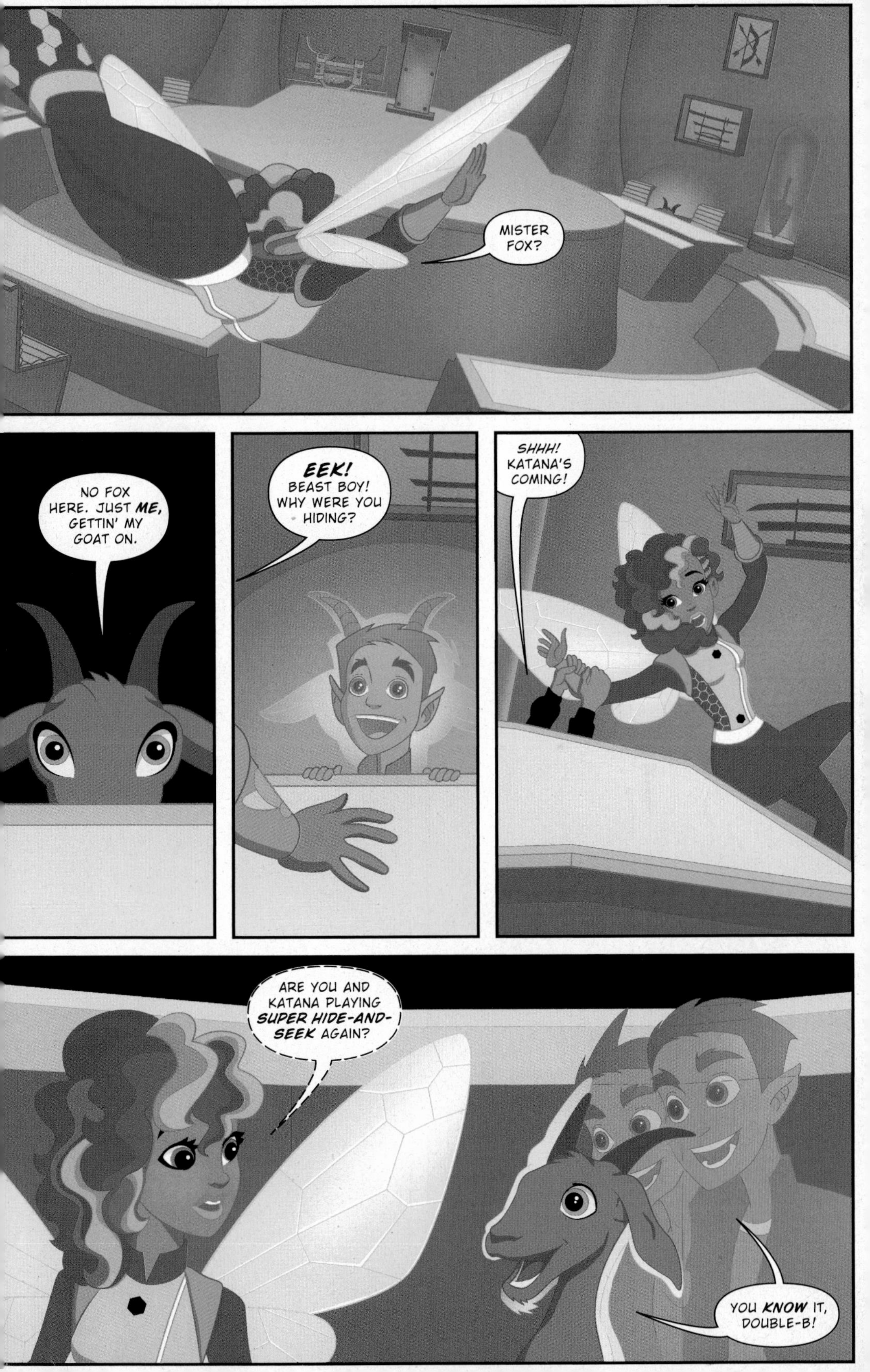

MISTER FOX?
NO FOX HERE. JUST **ME,** GETTIN' MY GOAT ON.
EEK! BEAST BOY! WHY WERE YOU HIDING?
SHHH! KATANA'S COMING!
ARE YOU AND KATANA PLAYING **SUPER HIDE-AND-SEEK** AGAIN?
YOU **KNOW** IT, DOUBLE-B!

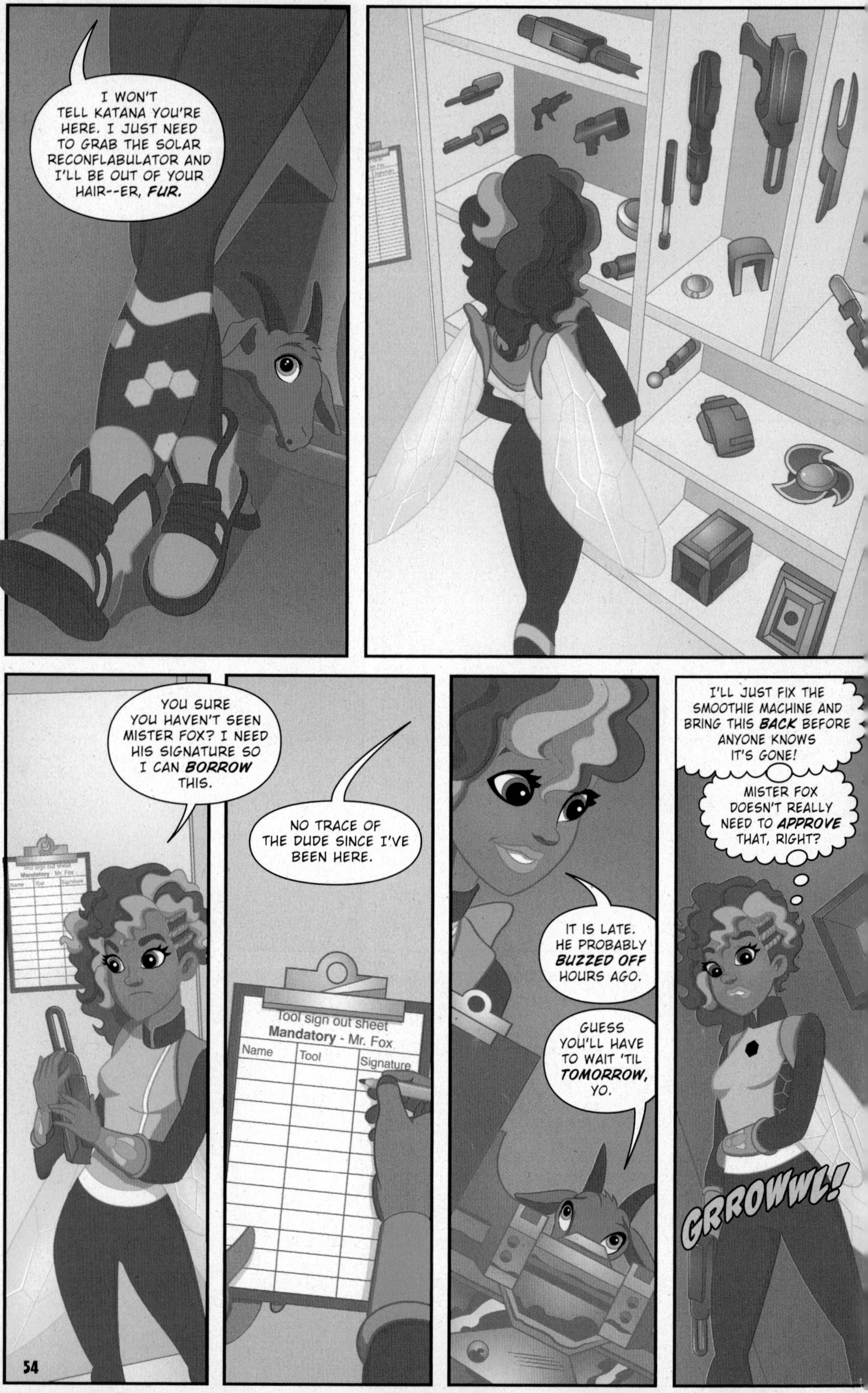
I WON'T TELL KATANA YOU'RE HERE. I JUST NEED TO GRAB THE SOLAR RECONFLABULATOR AND I'LL BE OUT OF YOUR HAIR--ER, **FUR.**
YOU SURE YOU HAVEN'T SEEN MISTER FOX? I NEED HIS SIGNATURE SO I CAN **BORROW** THIS.
NO TRACE OF THE DUDE SINCE I'VE BEEN HERE.
Tool sign out sheet
Mandatory - Mr. Fox
Name
Tool
Signature
IT IS LATE. HE PROBABLY **BUZZED OFF** HOURS AGO.
GUESS YOU'LL HAVE TO WAIT 'TIL **TOMORROW,** YO.
I'LL JUST FIX THE SMOOTHIE MACHINE AND BRING THIS **BACK** BEFORE ANYONE KNOWS IT'S GONE!
MISTER FOX DOESN'T REALLY NEED TO **APPROVE** THAT, RIGHT?
GRROWWL!

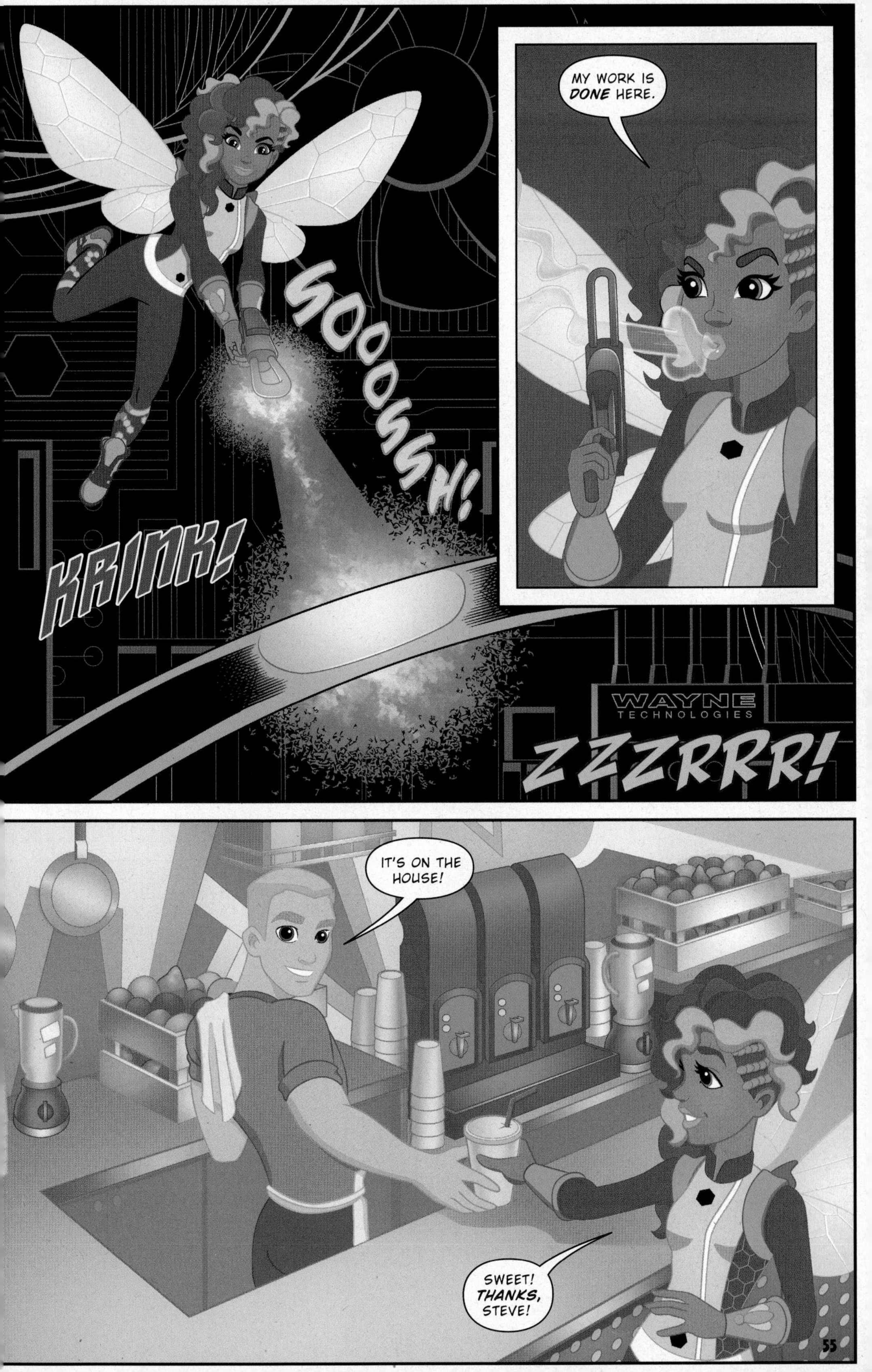
SOOOOSSSH!
KRINK!
MY WORK IS DONE HERE.
WAYNE TECHNOLOGIES
ZZZRRR!
IT'S ON THE HOUSE!
SWEET! THANKS, STEVE!

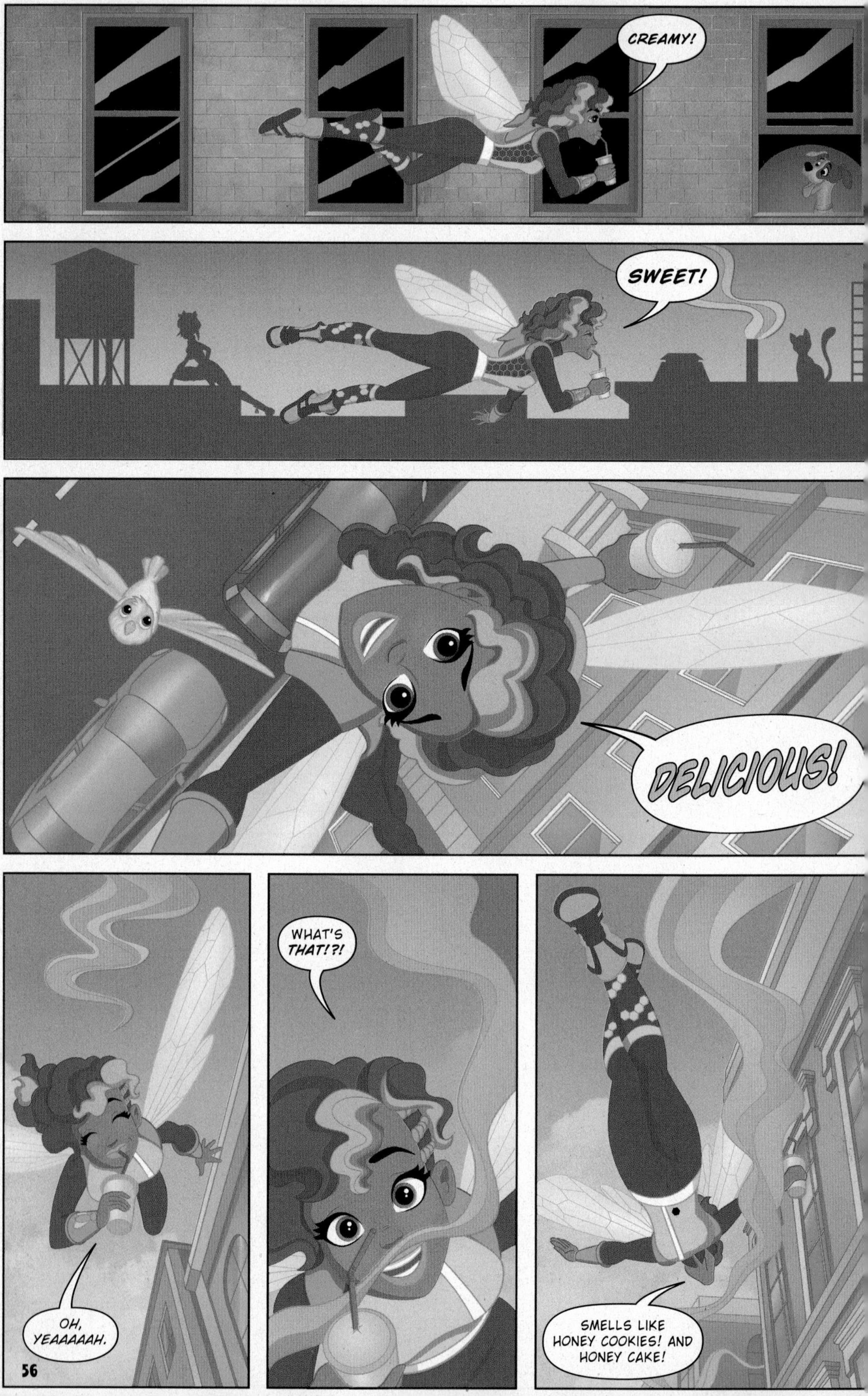
CREAMY!
SWEET!
DELICIOUS!
OH, YEAAAAAH.
WHAT'S THAT!?!
SMELLS LIKE HONEY COOKIES! AND HONEY CAKE!

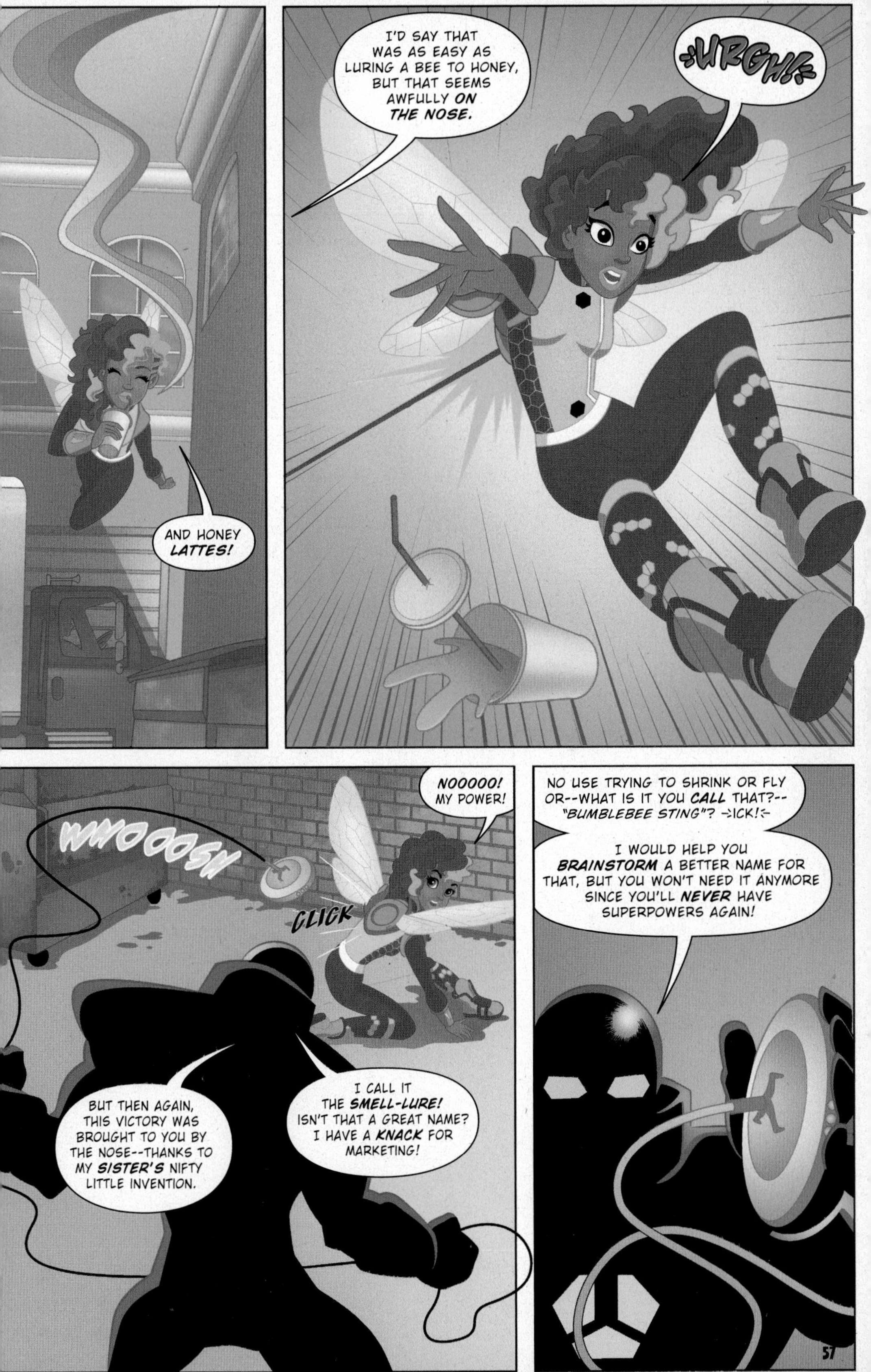
AND HONEY LATTES!
I'D SAY THAT WAS AS EASY AS LURING A BEE TO HONEY, BUT THAT SEEMS AWFULLY ON THE NOSE.
URGH!
WHOOOSH
NOOOOO! MY POWER!
CLICK
BUT THEN AGAIN, THIS VICTORY WAS BROUGHT TO YOU BY THE NOSE--THANKS TO MY SISTER'S NIFTY LITTLE INVENTION.
I CALL IT THE SMELL-LURE! ISN'T THAT A GREAT NAME? I HAVE A KNACK FOR MARKETING!
NO USE TRYING TO SHRINK OR FLY OR--WHAT IS IT YOU CALL THAT?--"BUMBLEBEE STING"? ICK!
I WOULD HELP YOU BRAINSTORM A BETTER NAME FOR THAT, BUT YOU WON'T NEED IT ANYMORE SINCE YOU'LL NEVER HAVE SUPERPOWERS AGAIN!

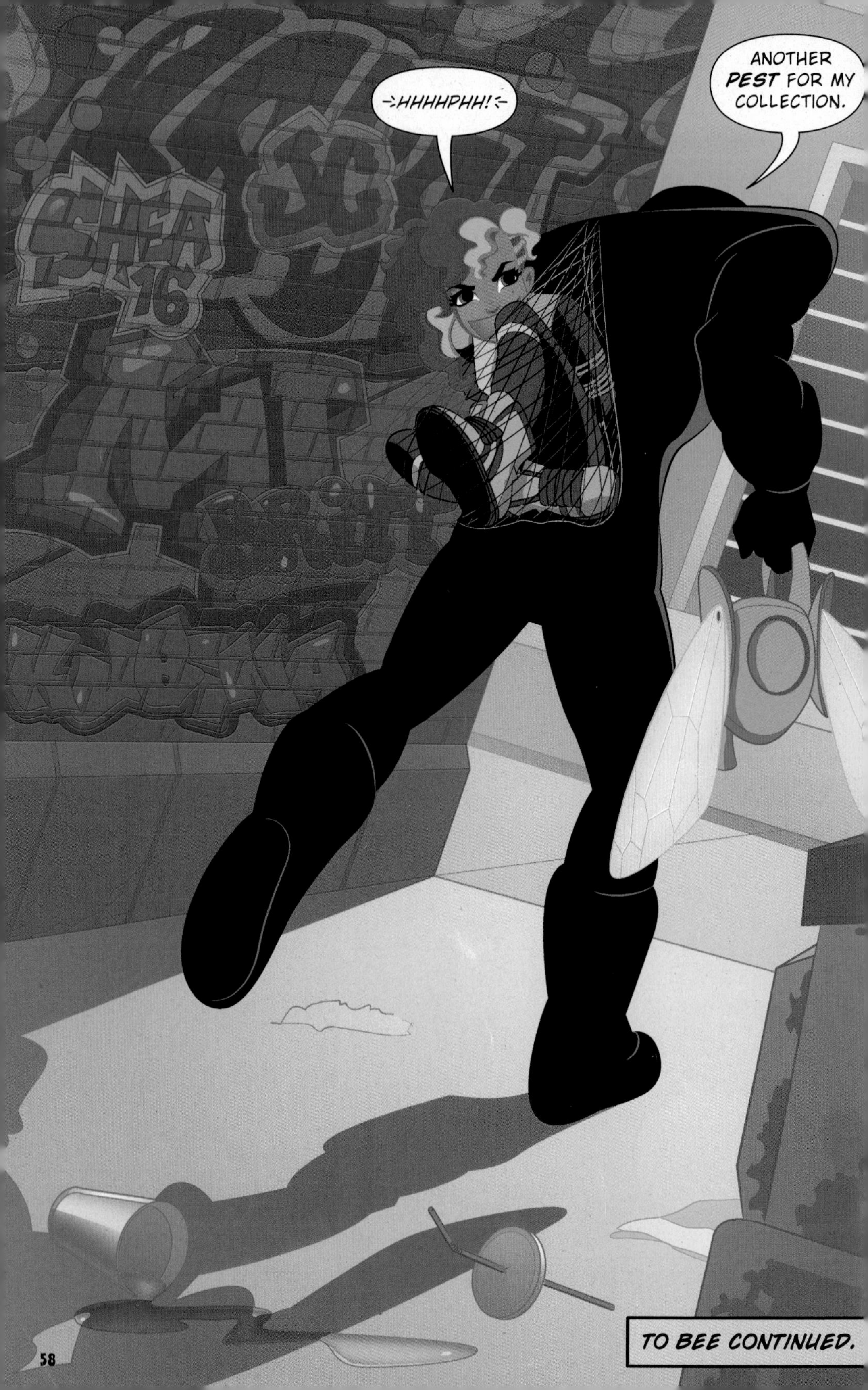

-HHHHPHH!-
ANOTHER **PEST** FOR MY COLLECTION.
TO BEE CONTINUED.

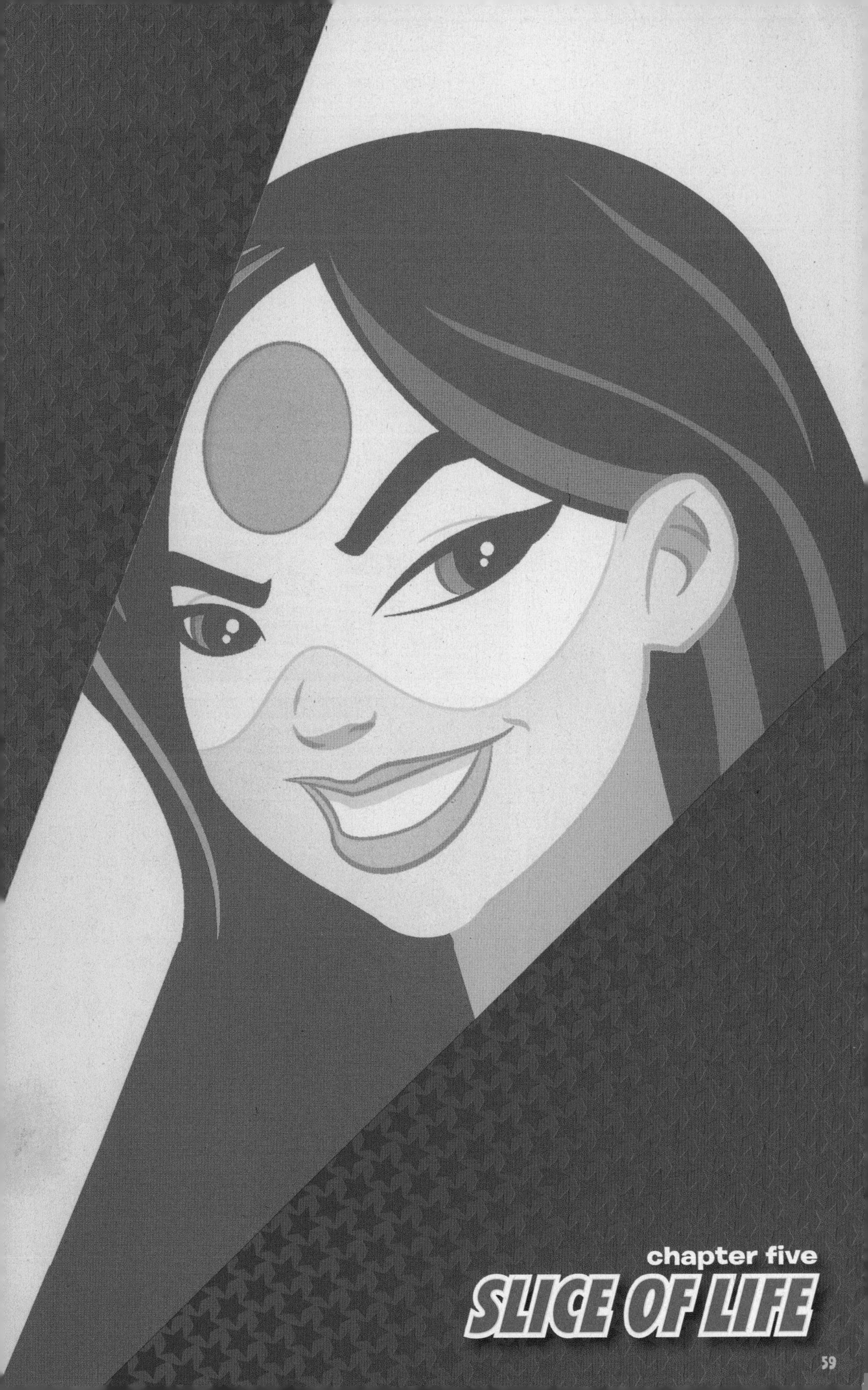

chapter five

SLICE OF LIFE

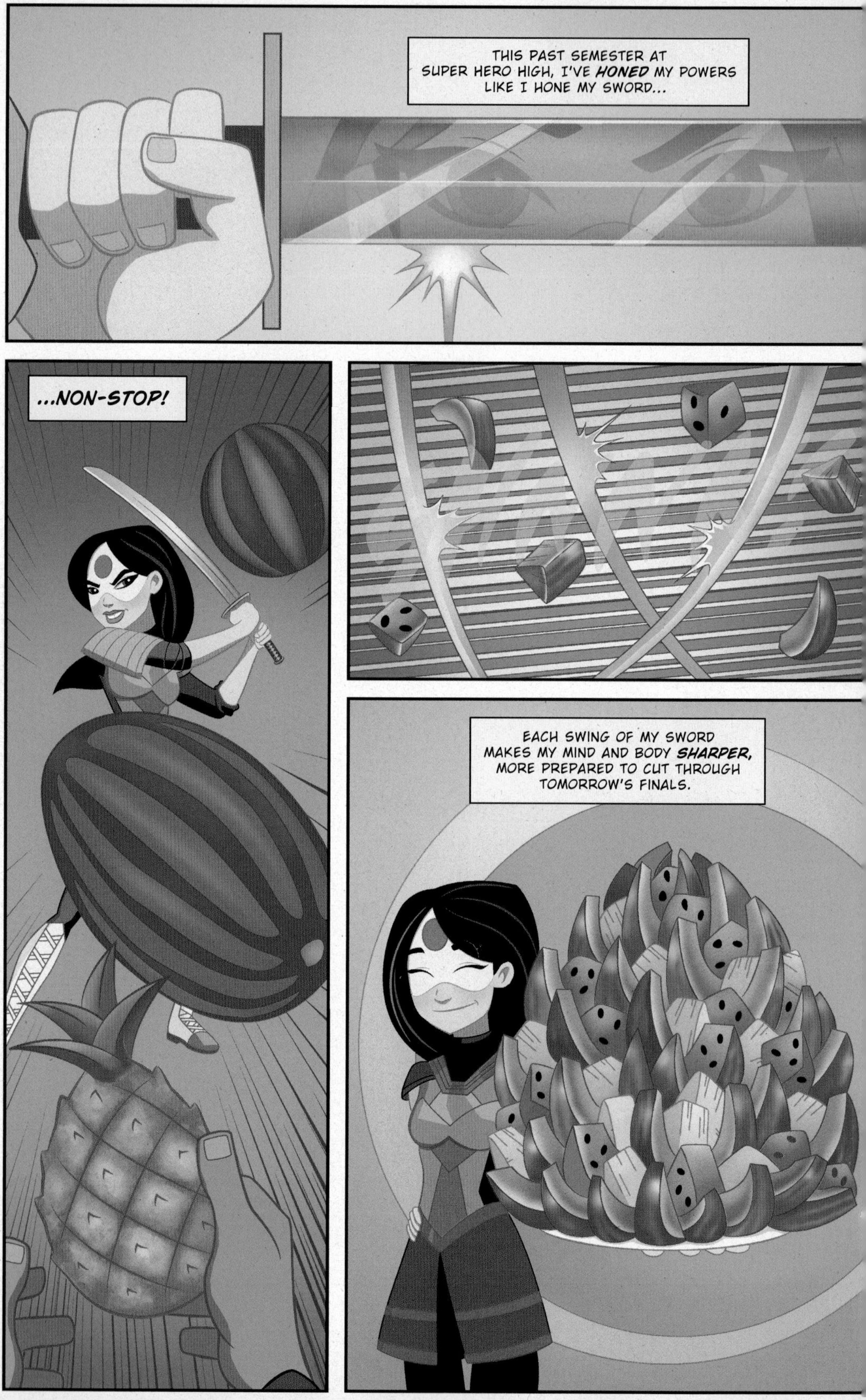
THIS PAST SEMESTER AT SUPER HERO HIGH, I'VE HONED MY POWERS LIKE I HONE MY SWORD...
...NON-STOP!
EACH SWING OF MY SWORD MAKES MY MIND AND BODY SHARPER, MORE PREPARED TO CUT THROUGH TOMORROW'S FINALS.

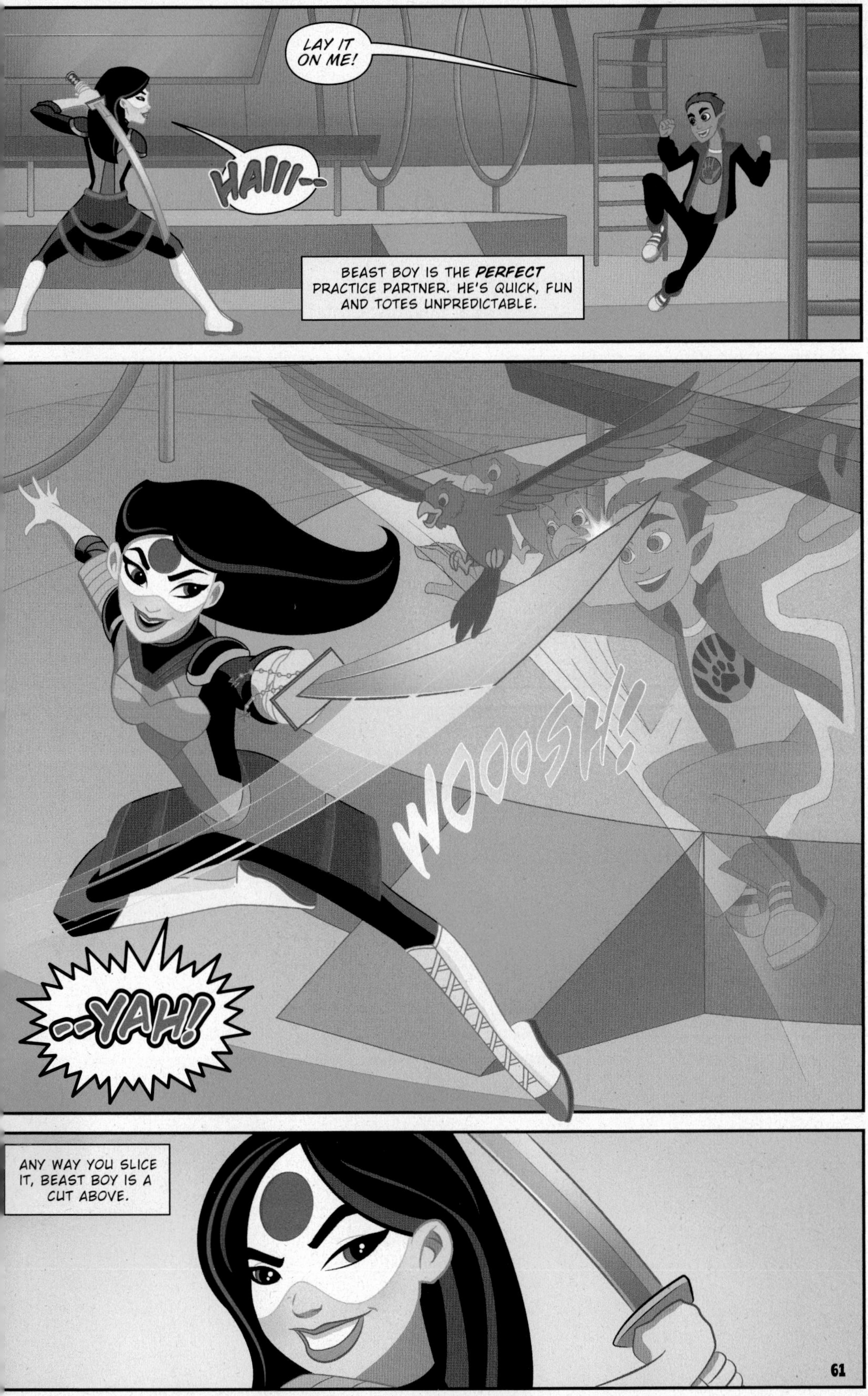
LAY IT ON ME!
HAIII--
BEAST BOY IS THE PERFECT PRACTICE PARTNER. HE'S QUICK, FUN AND TOTES UNPREDICTABLE.
WOOOSH!
--YAH!
ANY WAY YOU SLICE IT, BEAST BOY IS A CUT ABOVE.

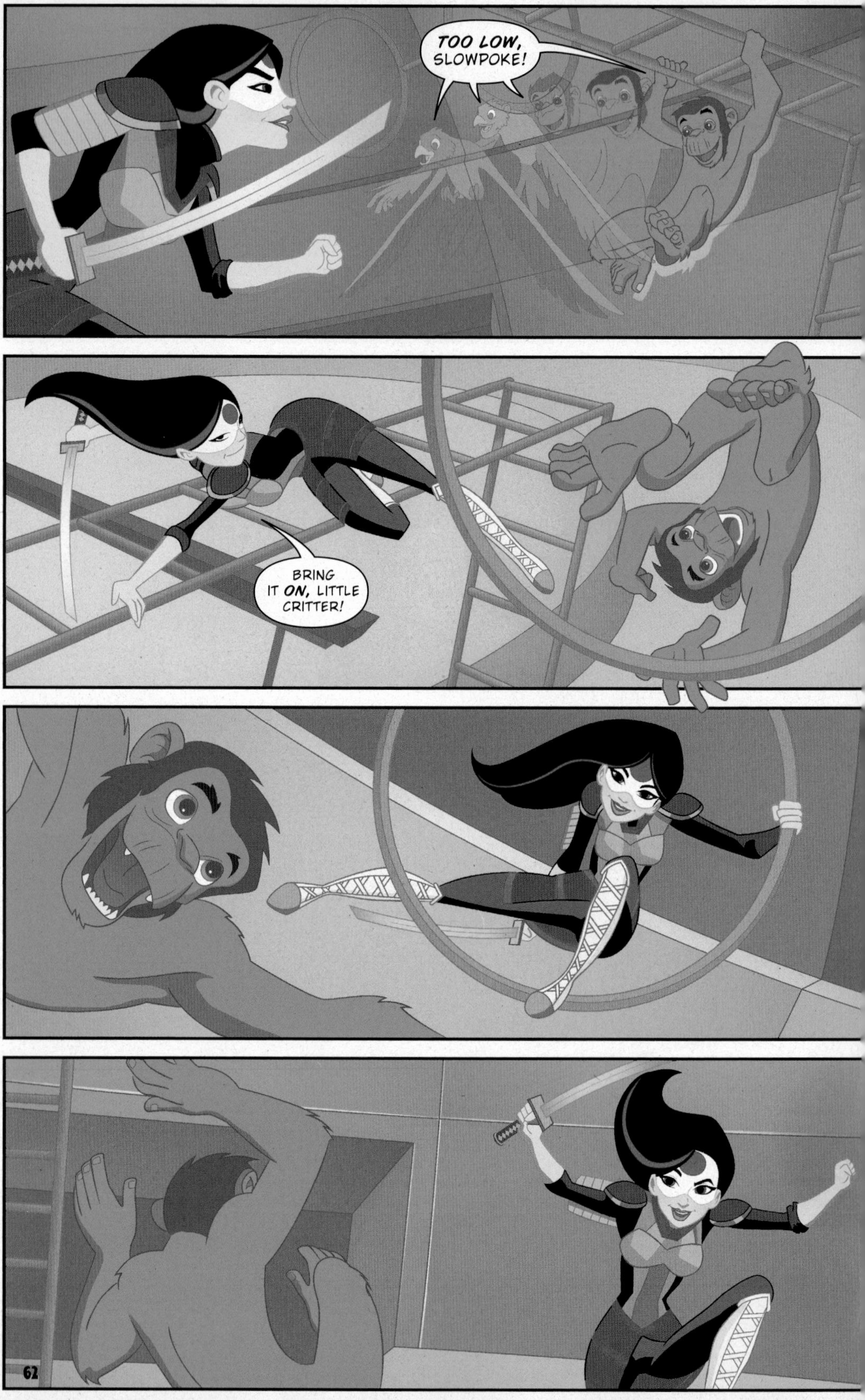
TOO LOW, SLOWPOKE!
BRING IT ON, LITTLE CRITTER!

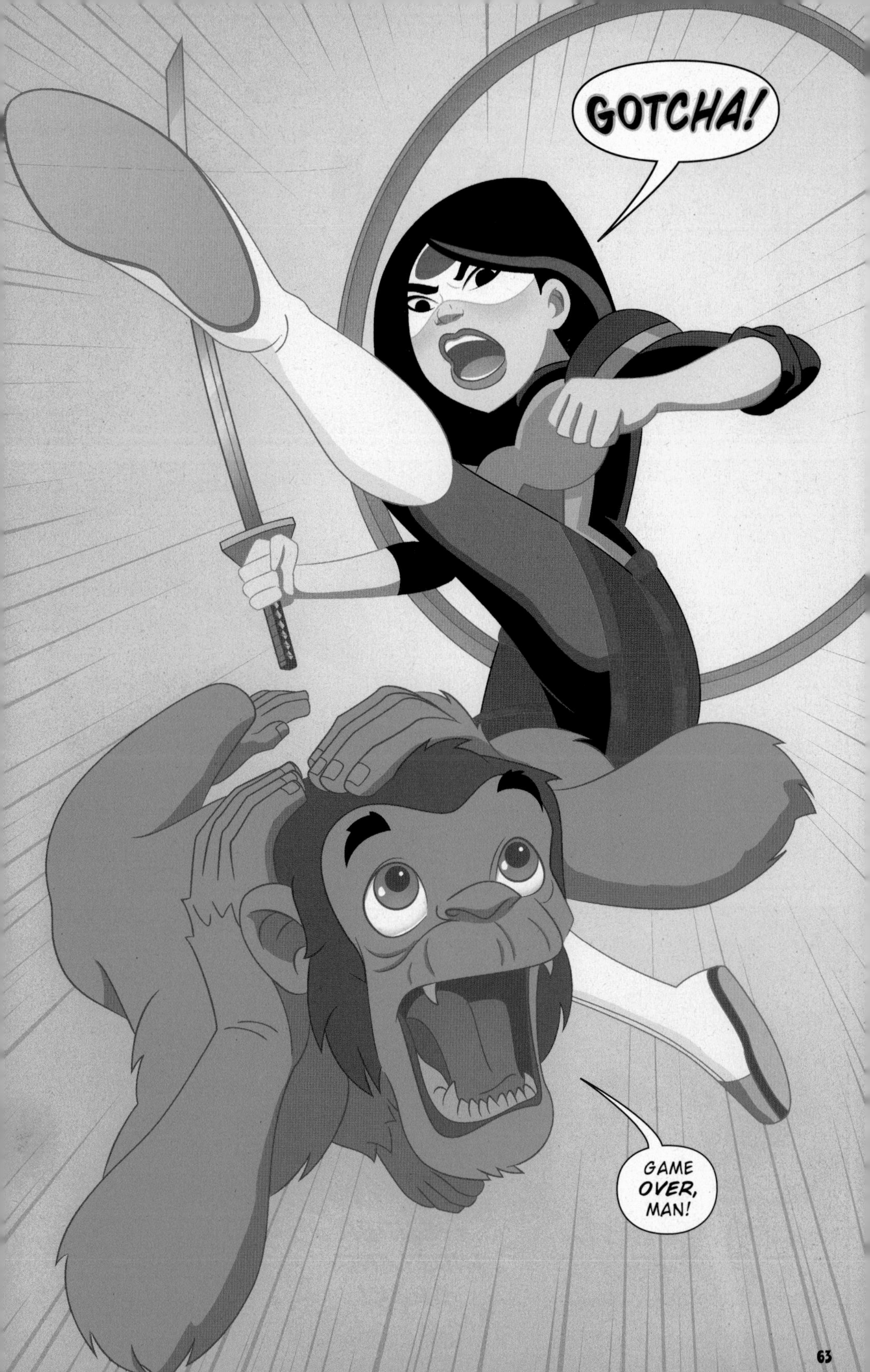
GOTCHA!
GAME OVER, MAN!

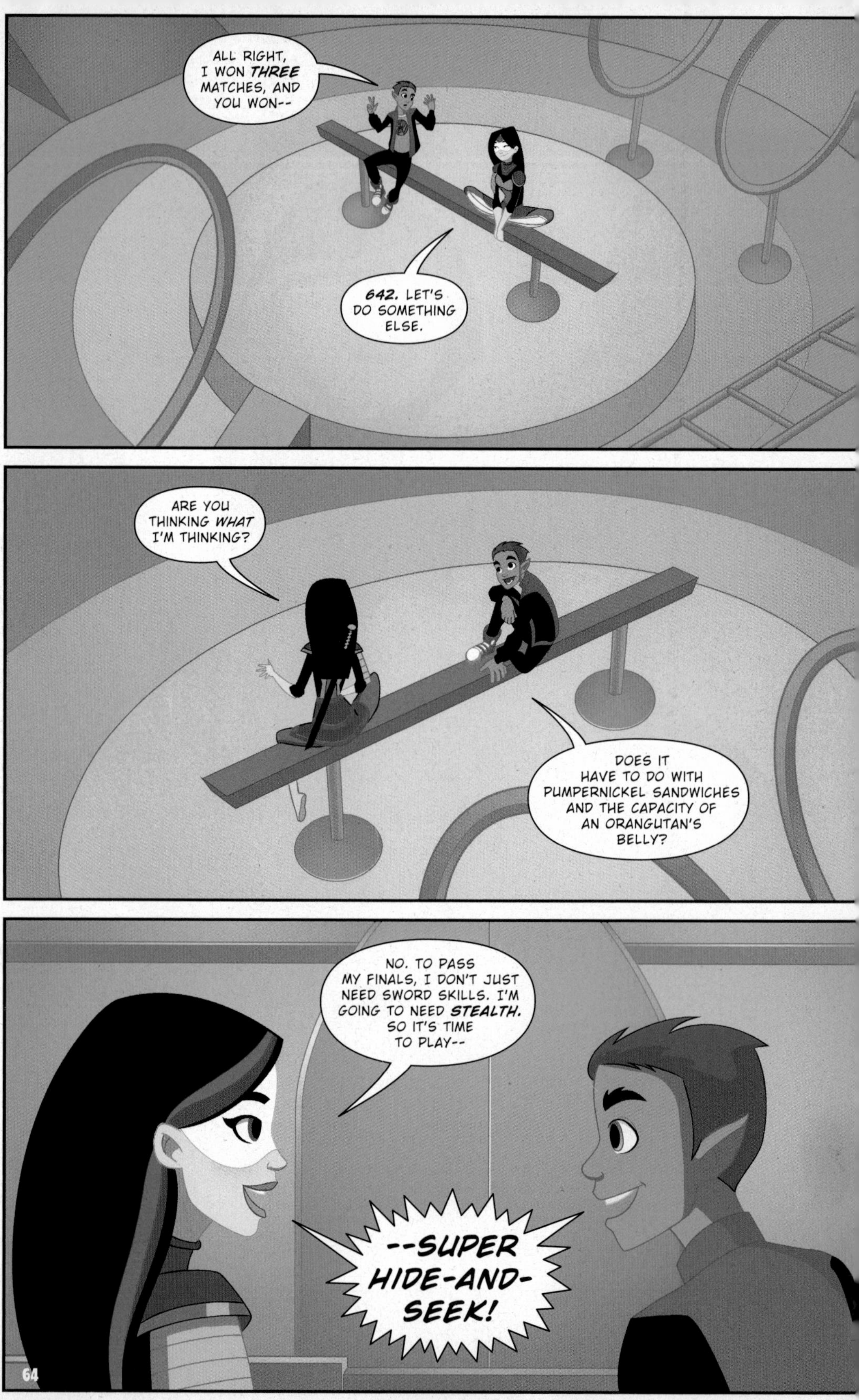
ALL RIGHT, I WON THREE MATCHES, AND YOU WON--
642. LET'S DO SOMETHING ELSE.
ARE YOU THINKING WHAT I'M THINKING?
DOES IT HAVE TO DO WITH PUMPERNICKEL SANDWICHES AND THE CAPACITY OF AN ORANGUTAN'S BELLY?
NO. TO PASS MY FINALS, I DON'T JUST NEED SWORD SKILLS. I'M GOING TO NEED STEALTH. SO IT'S TIME TO PLAY--
--SUPER HIDE-AND-SEEK!

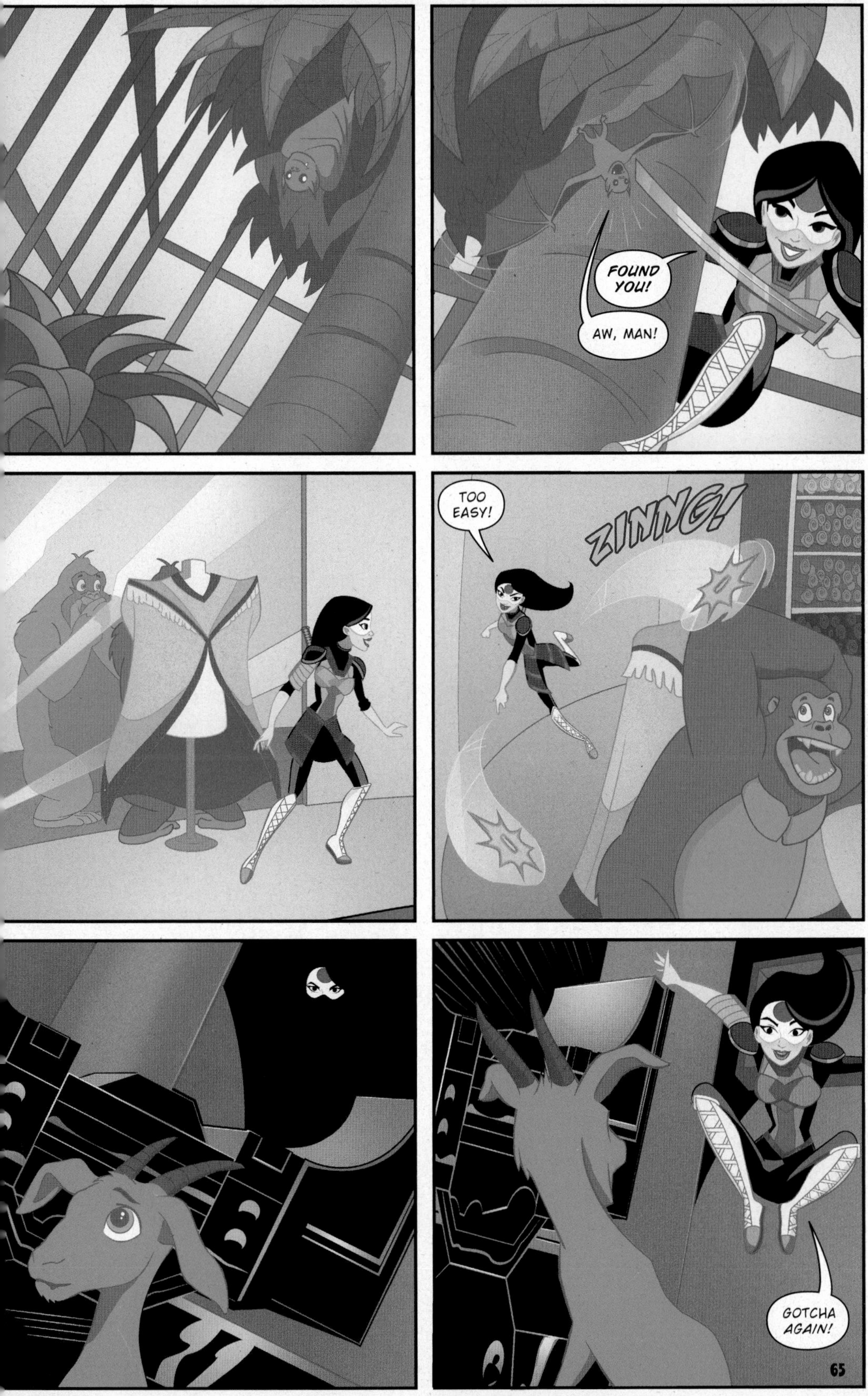
FOUND YOU!
AW, MAN!
TOO EASY!
ZINNG!
GOTCHA AGAIN!

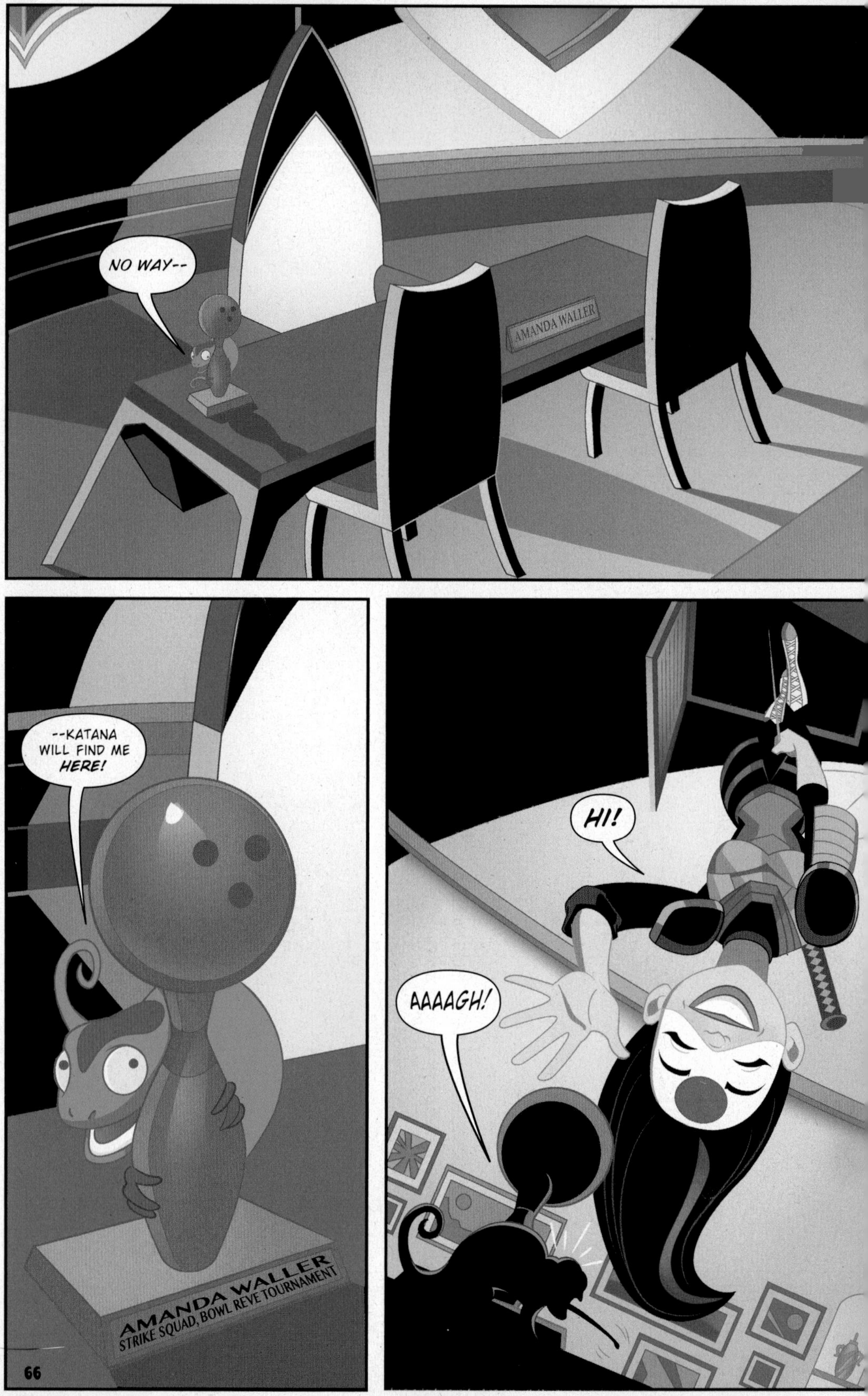
NO WAY--
AMANDA WALLER
--KATANA WILL FIND ME HERE!
AMANDA WALLER
STRIKE SQUAD, BOWL REVE TOURNAMENT
HI!
AAAAGH!

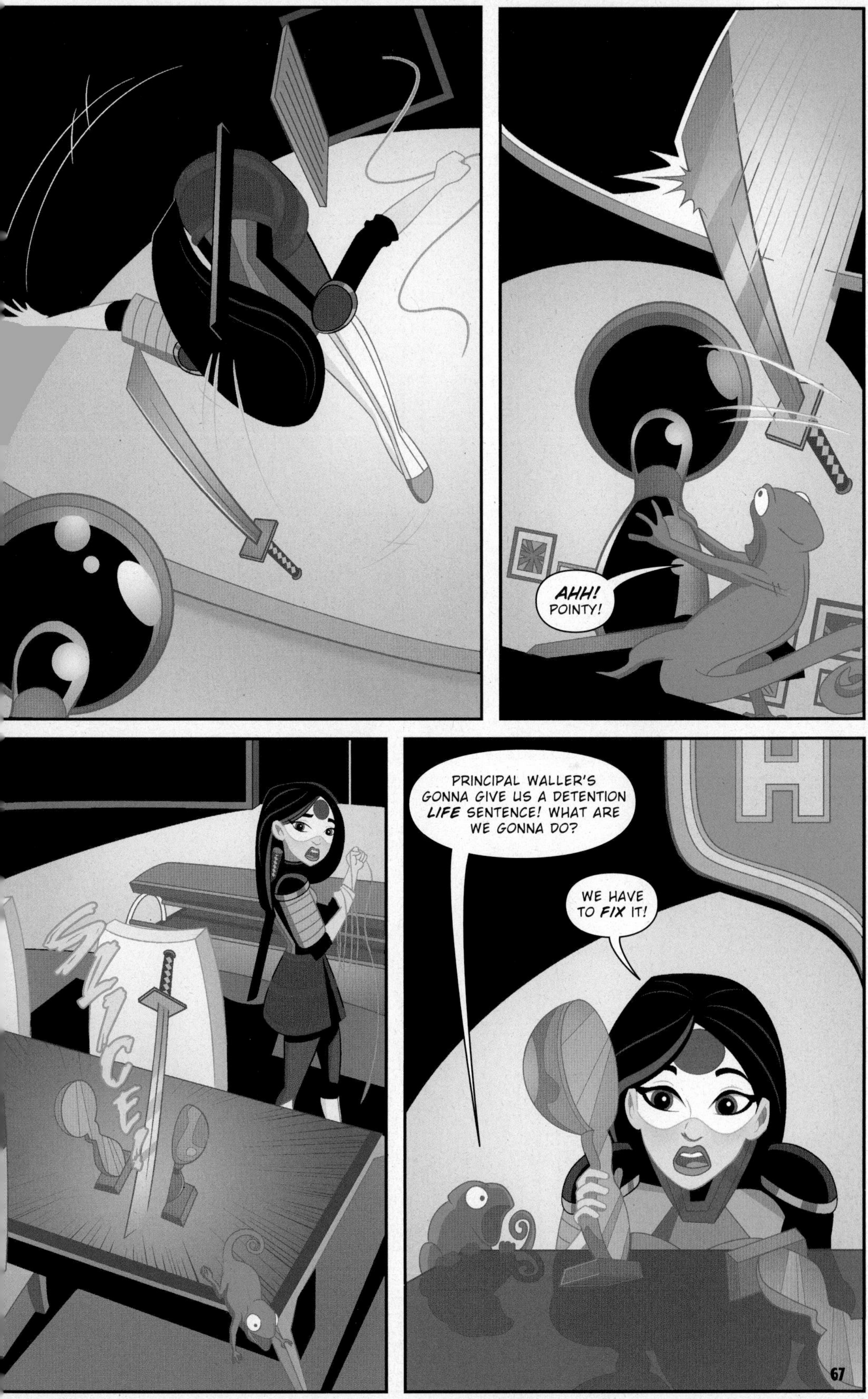
AHH! POINTY!
SLICE!
PRINCIPAL WALLER'S GONNA GIVE US A DETENTION LIFE SENTENCE! WHAT ARE WE GONNA DO?
WE HAVE TO FIX IT!

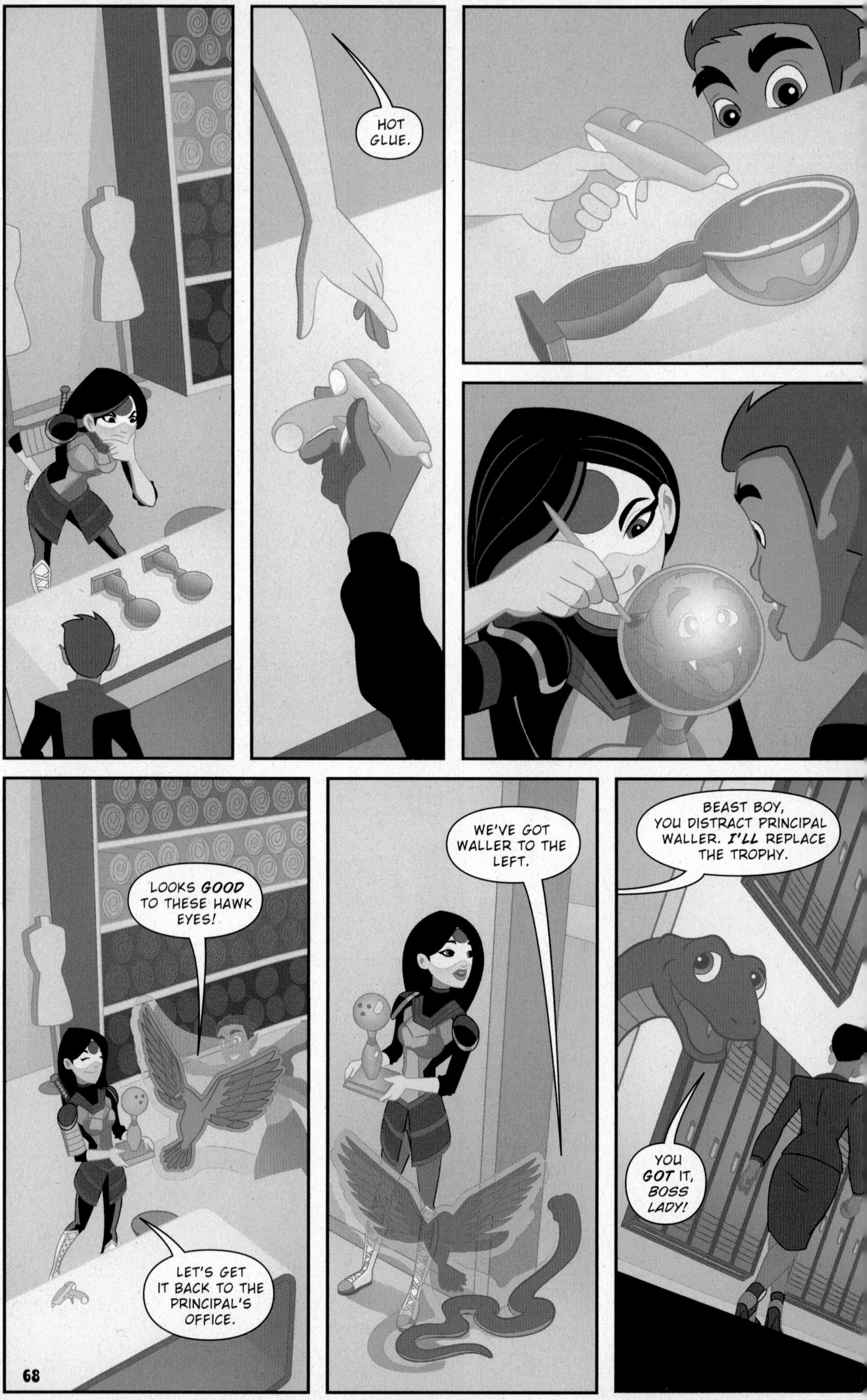
HOT GLUE.
LOOKS GOOD TO THESE HAWK EYES!
LET'S GET IT BACK TO THE PRINCIPAL'S OFFICE.
WE'VE GOT WALLER TO THE LEFT.
BEAST BOY, YOU DISTRACT PRINCIPAL WALLER. I'LL REPLACE THE TROPHY.
YOU GOT IT, BOSS LADY!

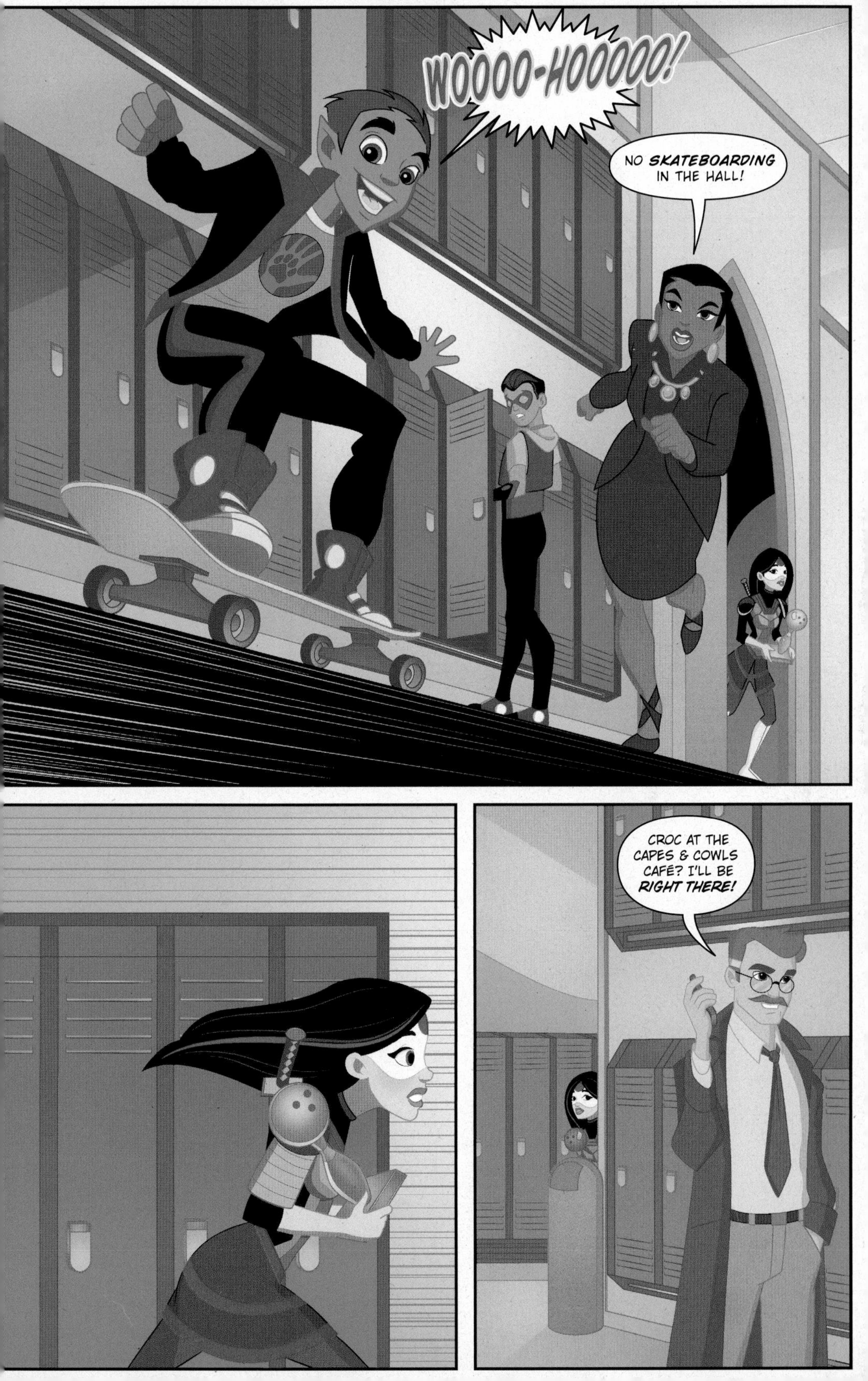
WOOOO-HOOOOO!
NO SKATEBOARDING IN THE HALL!
CROC AT THE CAPES & COWLS CAFÉ? I'LL BE RIGHT THERE!

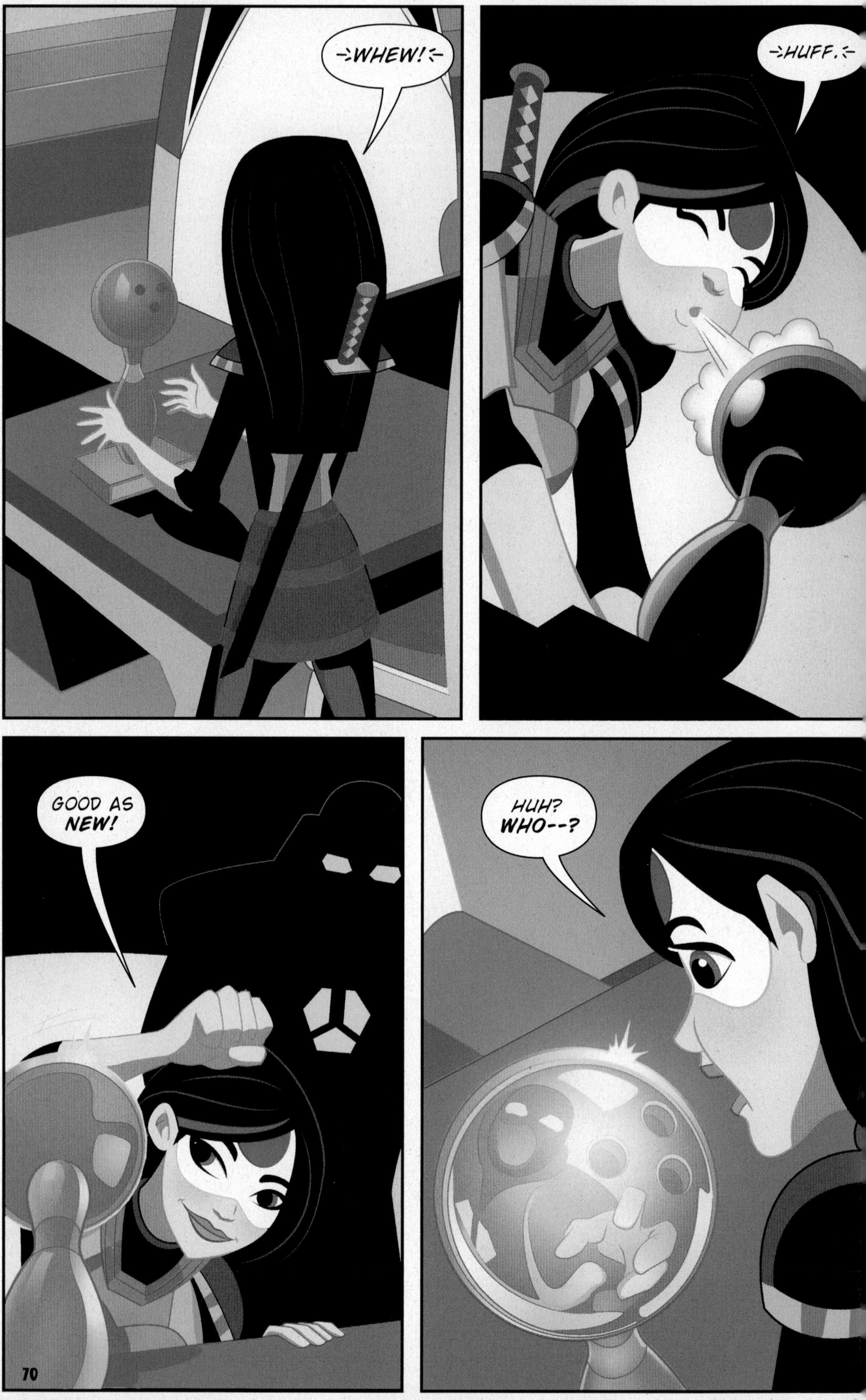
WHEW!
HUFF.
GOOD AS NEW!
HUH? WHO--?

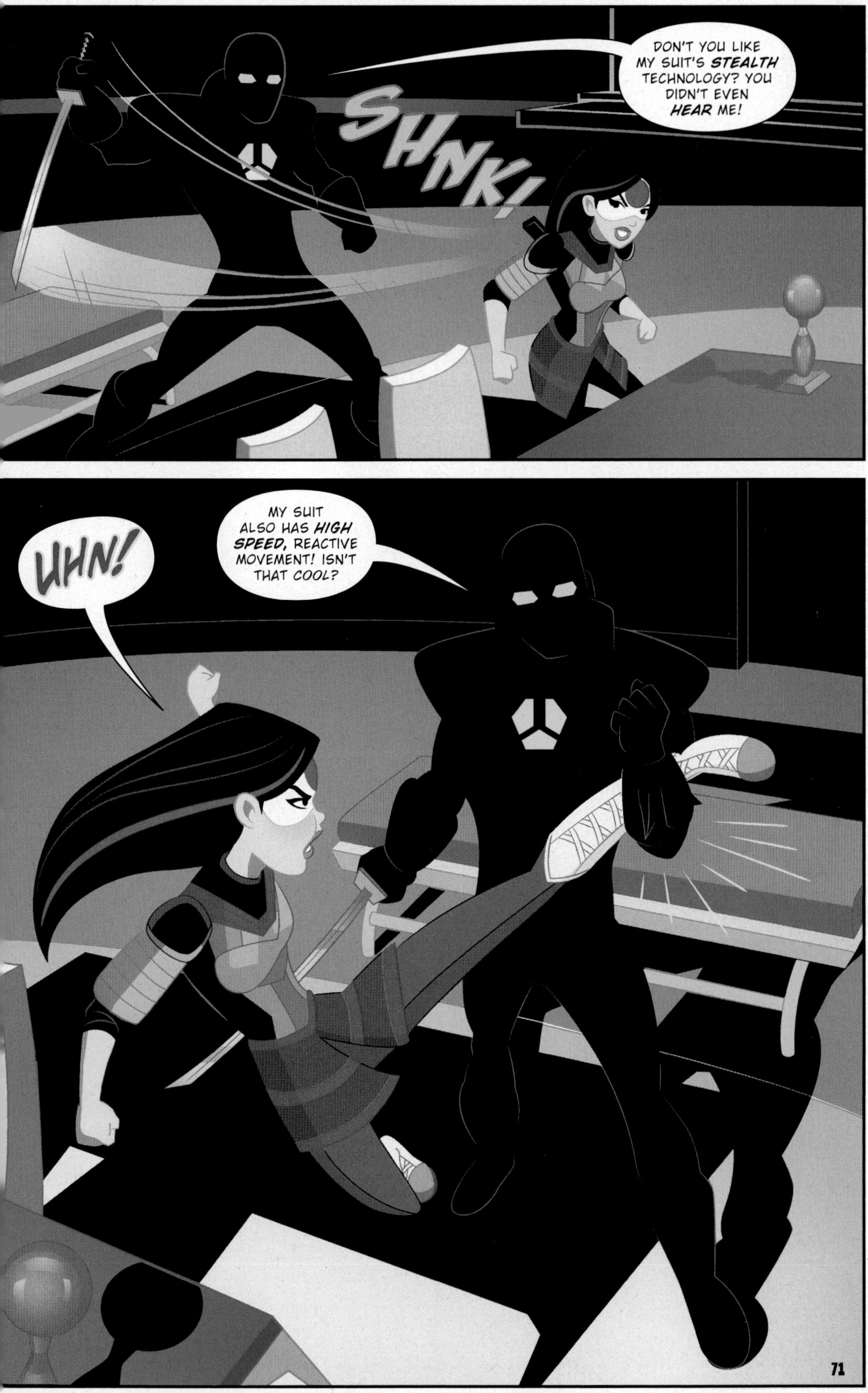
DON'T YOU LIKE MY SUIT'S STEALTH TECHNOLOGY? YOU DIDN'T EVEN HEAR ME!
SHNK!
MY SUIT ALSO HAS HIGH SPEED, REACTIVE MOVEMENT! ISN'T THAT COOL?
UHN!

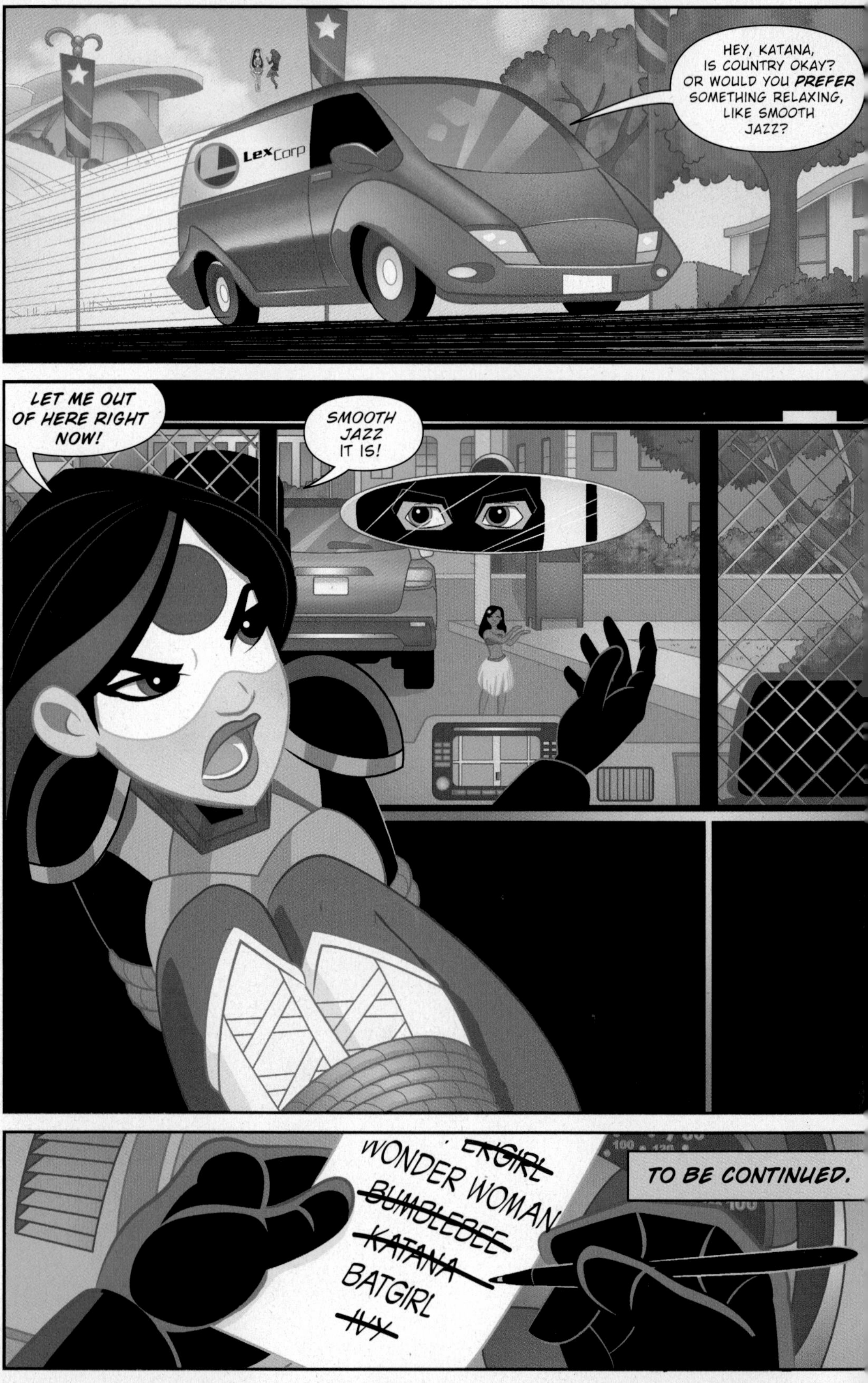
HEY, KATANA, IS COUNTRY OKAY? OR WOULD YOU *PREFER* SOMETHING RELAXING, LIKE SMOOTH JAZZ?
Lex Corp
LET ME OUT OF HERE RIGHT NOW!
SMOOTH JAZZ IT IS!
WONDER WOMAN
~~BUMBLEBEE~~
~~KATANA~~
BATGIRL
~~IVY~~
TO BE CONTINUED.

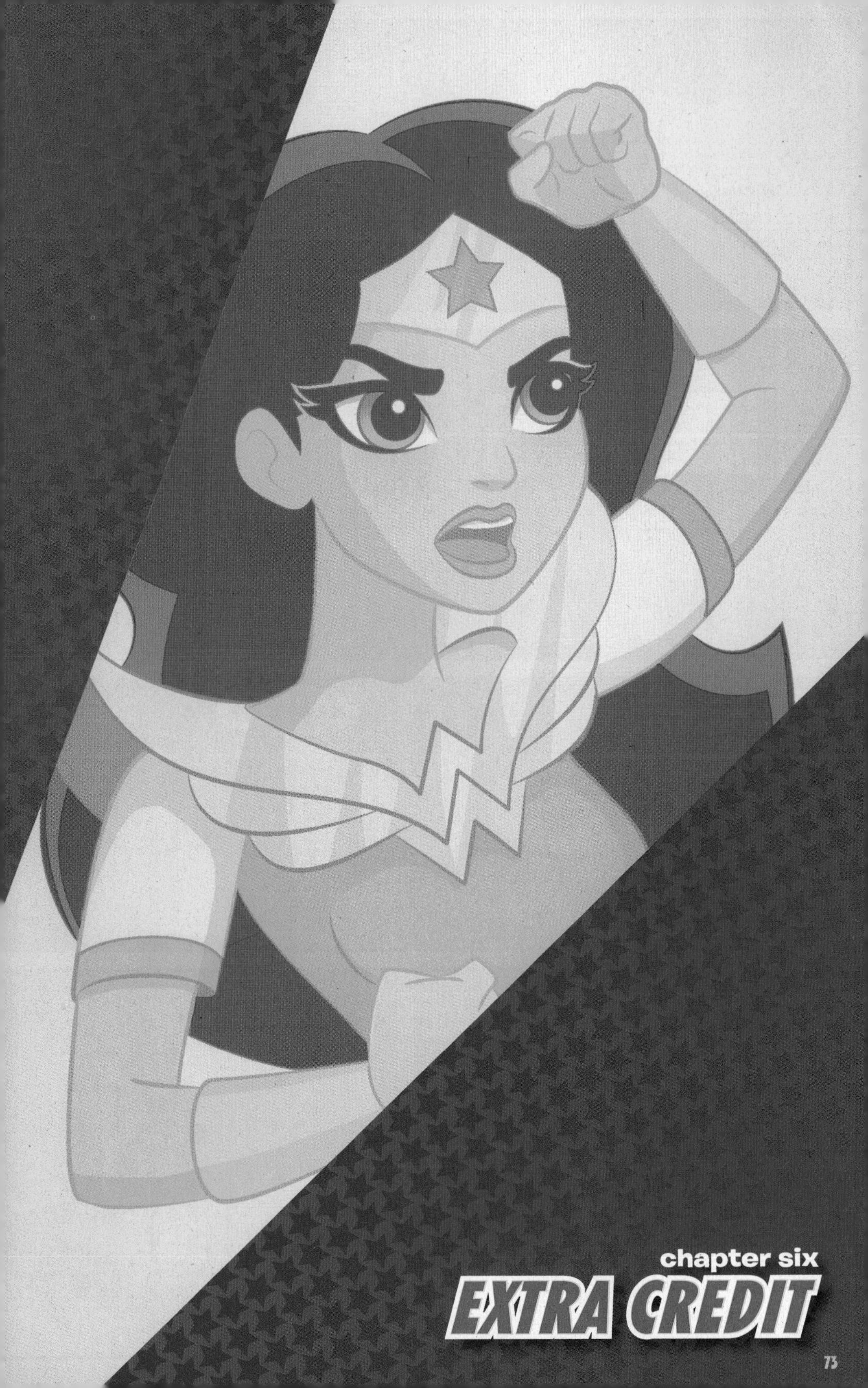

chapter six

EXTRA CREDIT

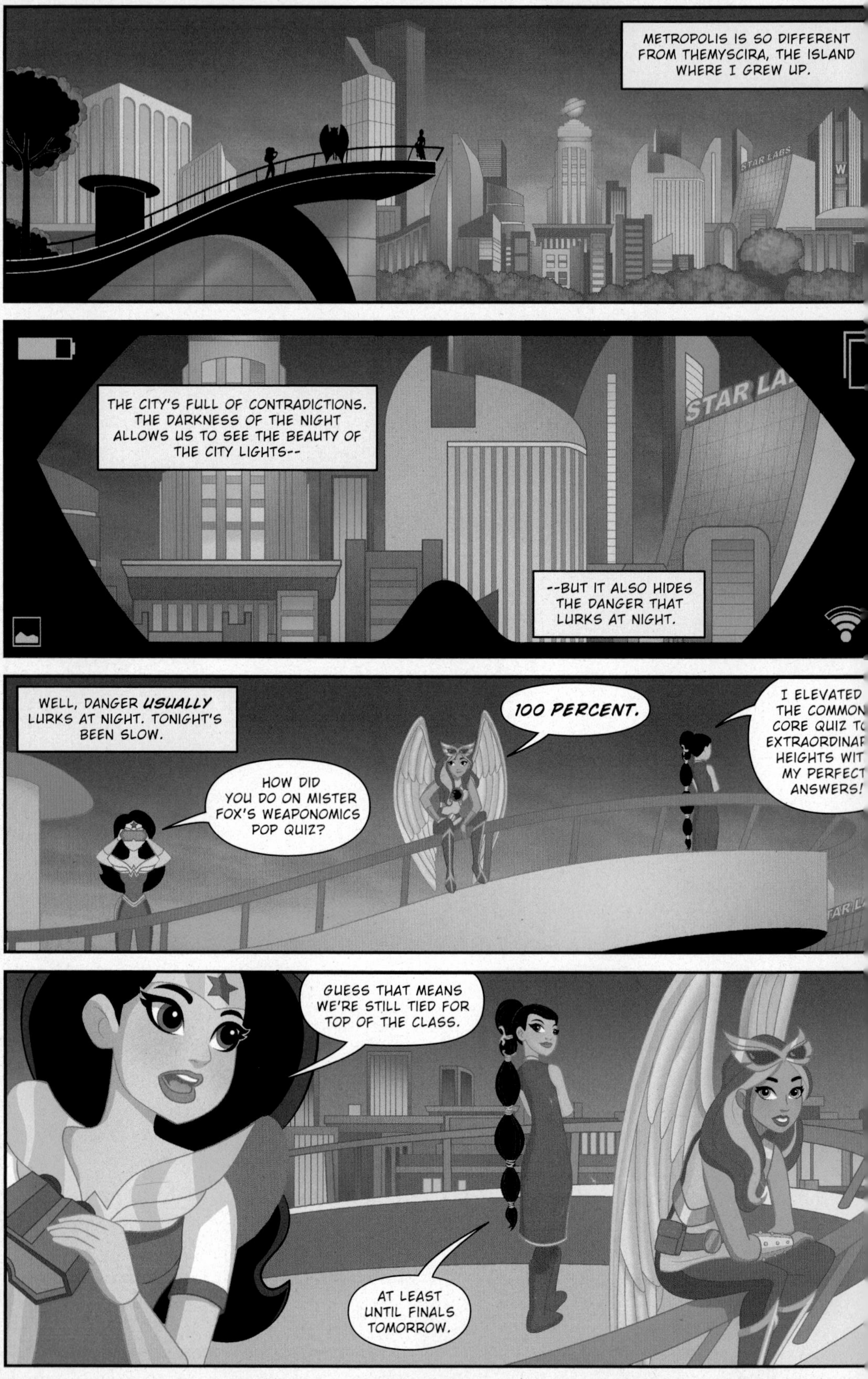
METROPOLIS IS SO DIFFERENT FROM THEMYSCIRA, THE ISLAND WHERE I GREW UP.
STAR LABS
THE CITY'S FULL OF CONTRADICTIONS. THE DARKNESS OF THE NIGHT ALLOWS US TO SEE THE BEAUTY OF THE CITY LIGHTS--
--BUT IT ALSO HIDES THE DANGER THAT LURKS AT NIGHT.
WELL, DANGER *USUALLY* LURKS AT NIGHT. TONIGHT'S BEEN SLOW.
HOW DID YOU DO ON MISTER FOX'S WEAPONOMICS POP QUIZ?
100 PERCENT.
I ELEVATED THE COMMON CORE QUIZ TO EXTRAORDINARY HEIGHTS WITH MY PERFECT ANSWERS!
GUESS THAT MEANS WE'RE STILL TIED FOR TOP OF THE CLASS.
AT LEAST UNTIL FINALS TOMORROW.

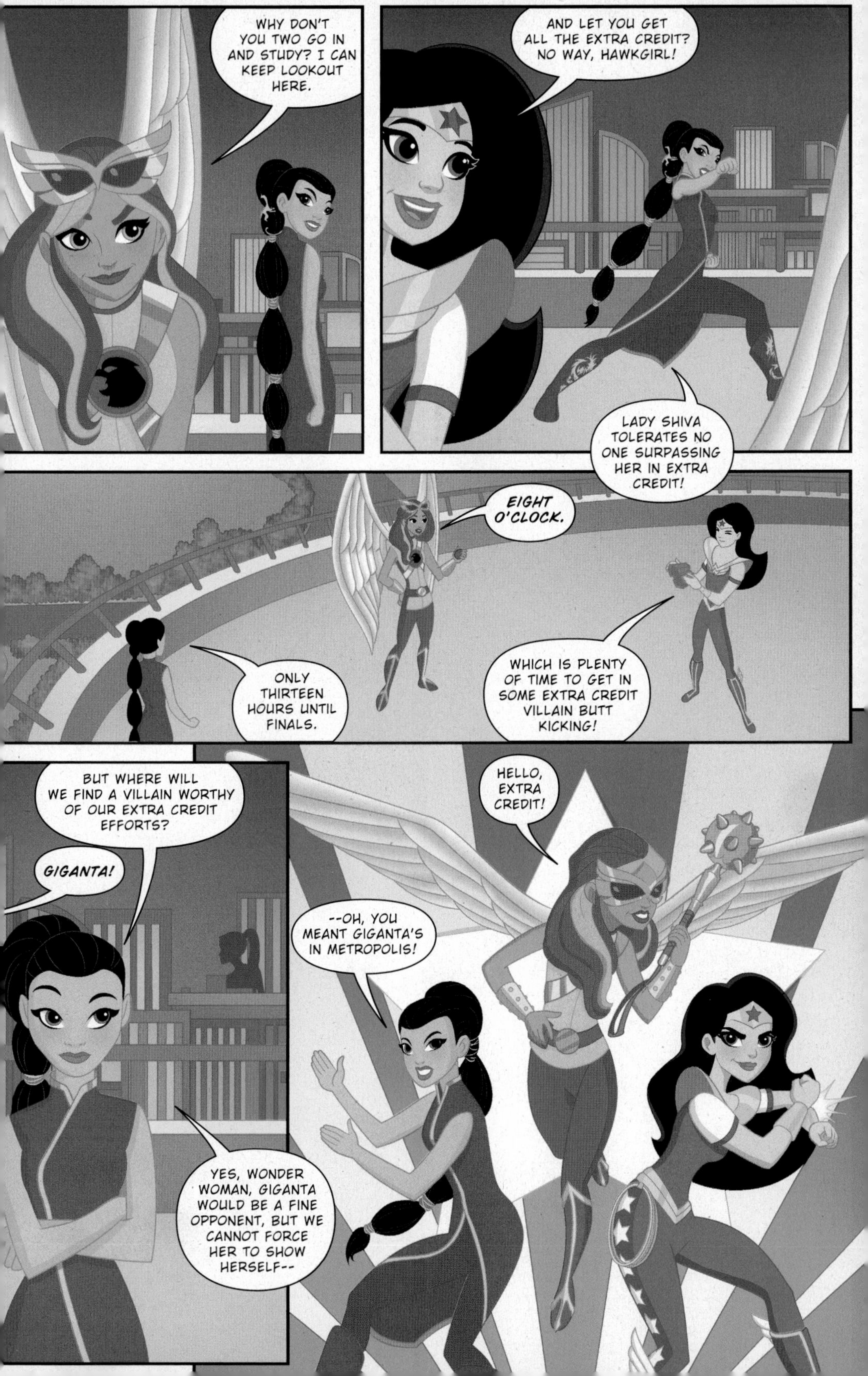
WHY DON'T YOU TWO GO IN AND STUDY? I CAN KEEP LOOKOUT HERE.
AND LET YOU GET ALL THE EXTRA CREDIT? NO WAY, HAWKGIRL!
LADY SHIVA TOLERATES NO ONE SURPASSING HER IN EXTRA CREDIT!
EIGHT O'CLOCK.
ONLY THIRTEEN HOURS UNTIL FINALS.
WHICH IS PLENTY OF TIME TO GET IN SOME EXTRA CREDIT VILLAIN BUTT KICKING!
BUT WHERE WILL WE FIND A VILLAIN WORTHY OF OUR EXTRA CREDIT EFFORTS?
GIGANTA!
YES, WONDER WOMAN, GIGANTA WOULD BE A FINE OPPONENT, BUT WE CANNOT FORCE HER TO SHOW HERSELF--
--OH, YOU MEANT GIGANTA'S IN METROPOLIS!
HELLO, EXTRA CREDIT!

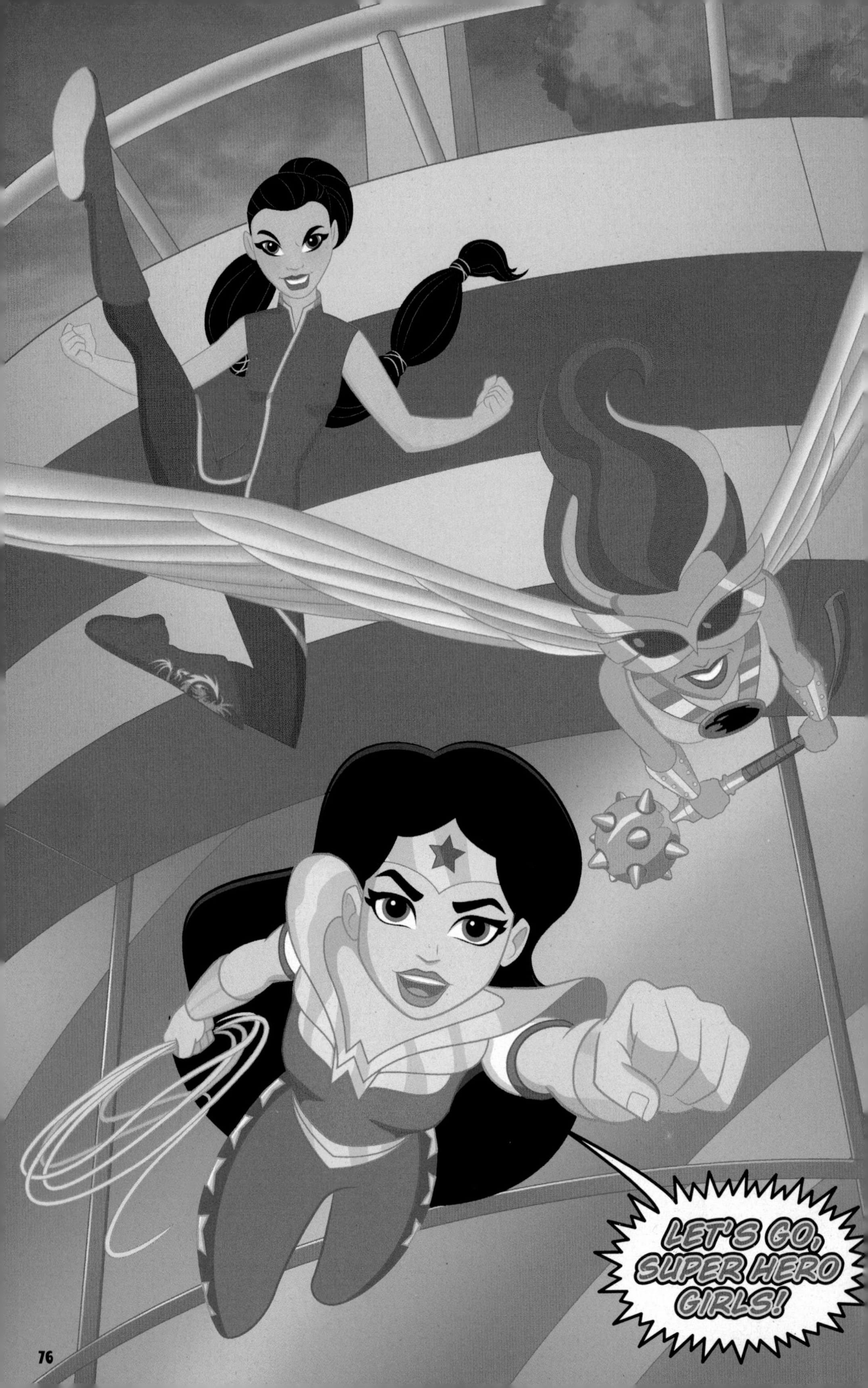
LET'S GO, SUPER HERO GIRLS!

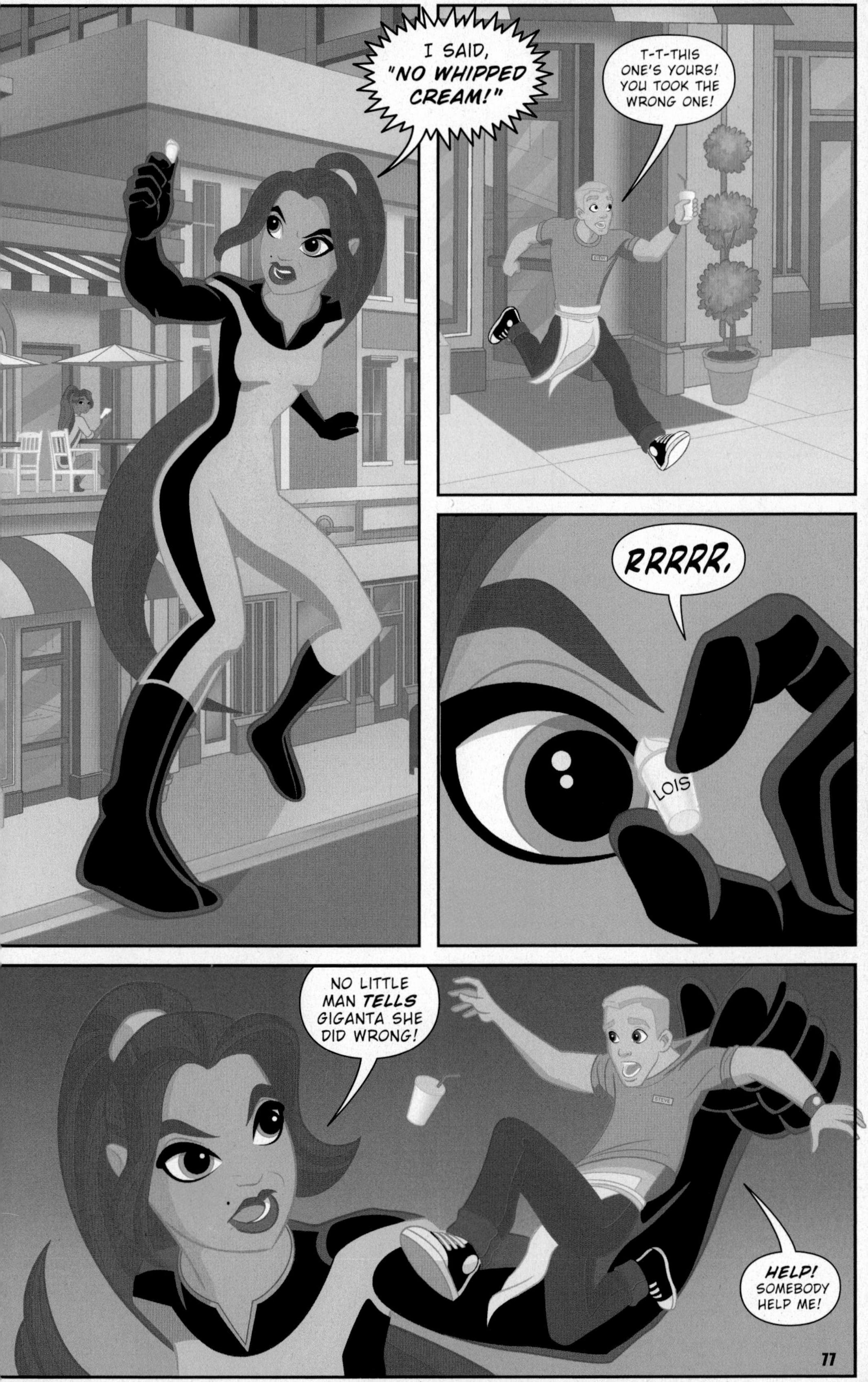
I SAID, "NO WHIPPED CREAM!"
T-T-THIS ONE'S YOURS! YOU TOOK THE WRONG ONE!
STEVE
RRRRR.
LOIS
NO LITTLE MAN TELLS GIGANTA SHE DID WRONG!
STEVE
HELP! SOMEBODY HELP ME!

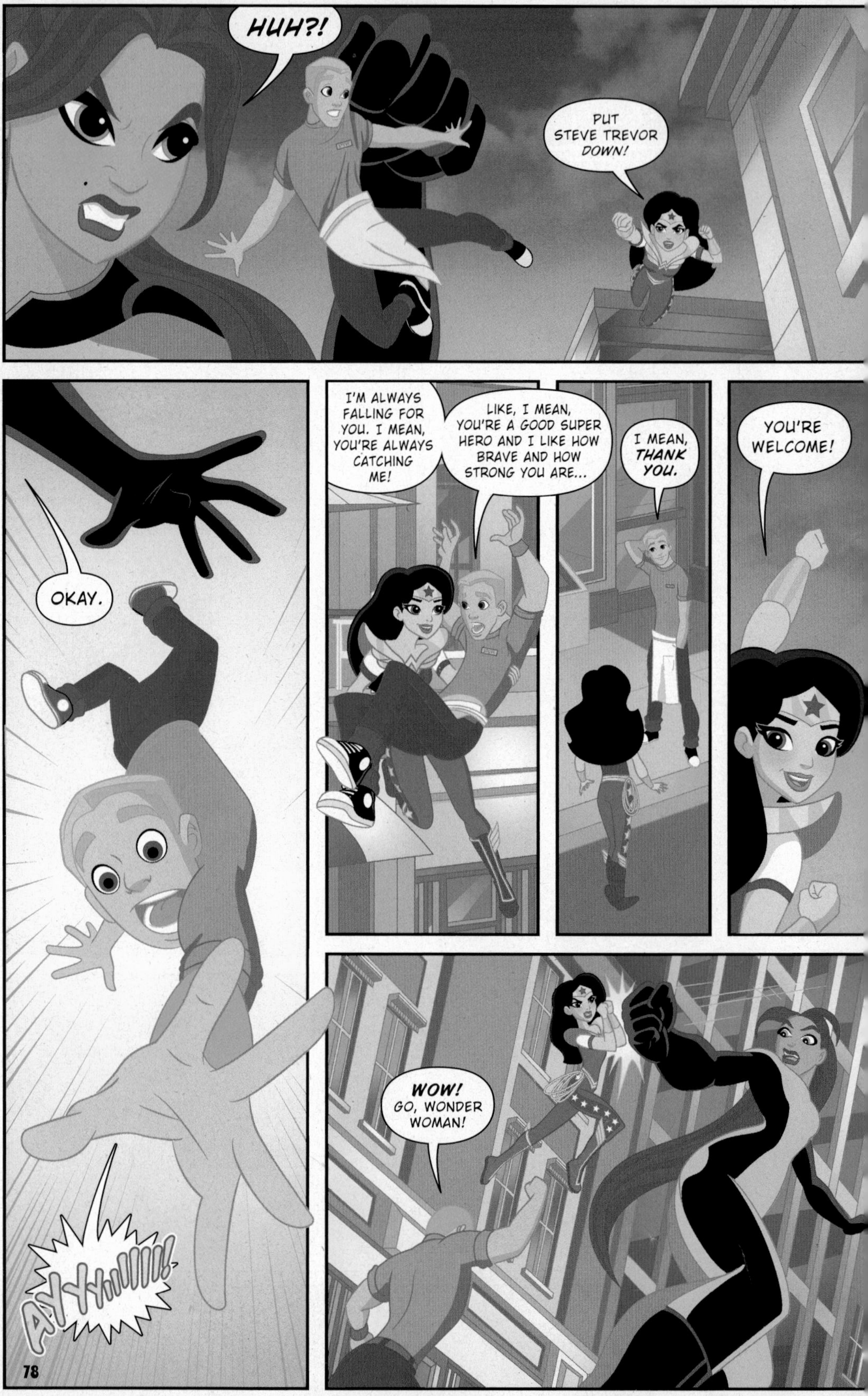
HUH?!
PUT STEVE TREVOR DOWN!
OKAY.
AYYYIIIIIII!
I'M ALWAYS FALLING FOR YOU. I MEAN, YOU'RE ALWAYS CATCHING ME!
LIKE, I MEAN, YOU'RE A GOOD SUPER HERO AND I LIKE HOW BRAVE AND HOW STRONG YOU ARE...
I MEAN, THANK YOU.
YOU'RE WELCOME!
WOW! GO, WONDER WOMAN!

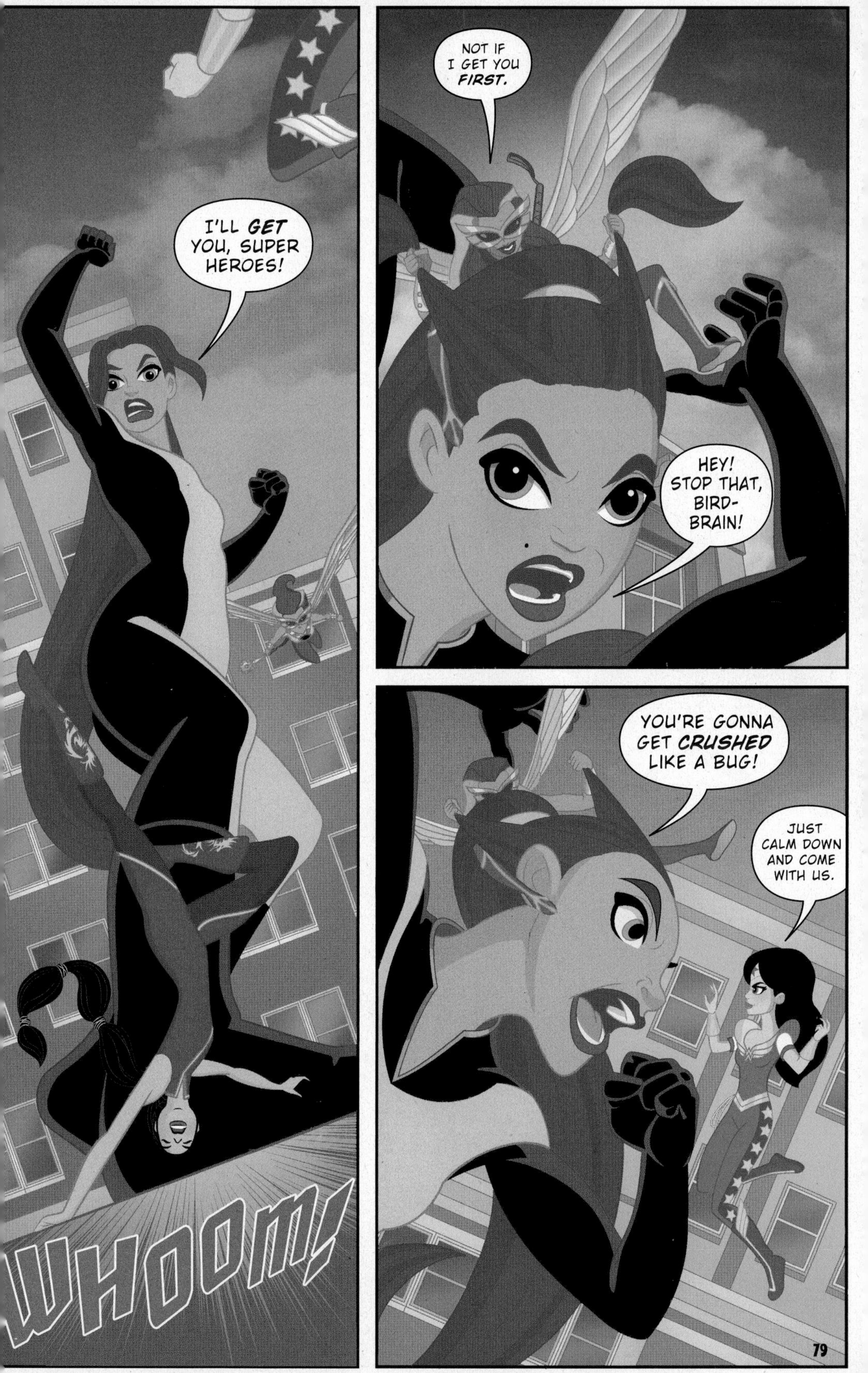
I'LL GET YOU, SUPER HEROES!
WHOOM!
NOT IF I GET YOU FIRST.
HEY! STOP THAT, BIRD-BRAIN!
YOU'RE GONNA GET CRUSHED LIKE A BUG!
JUST CALM DOWN AND COME WITH US.

WONDER WOMAN HAS BROUGHT OUT THE LASSO OF TRUTH!

FANS WILL RECALL THAT WONDER WOMAN HOLDS THE ALL-TIME LASSOING RECORD.

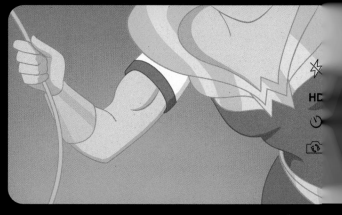

SHE AIMS FOR GIGANTA...

...AND SHE THROWS!

SWOOOSH

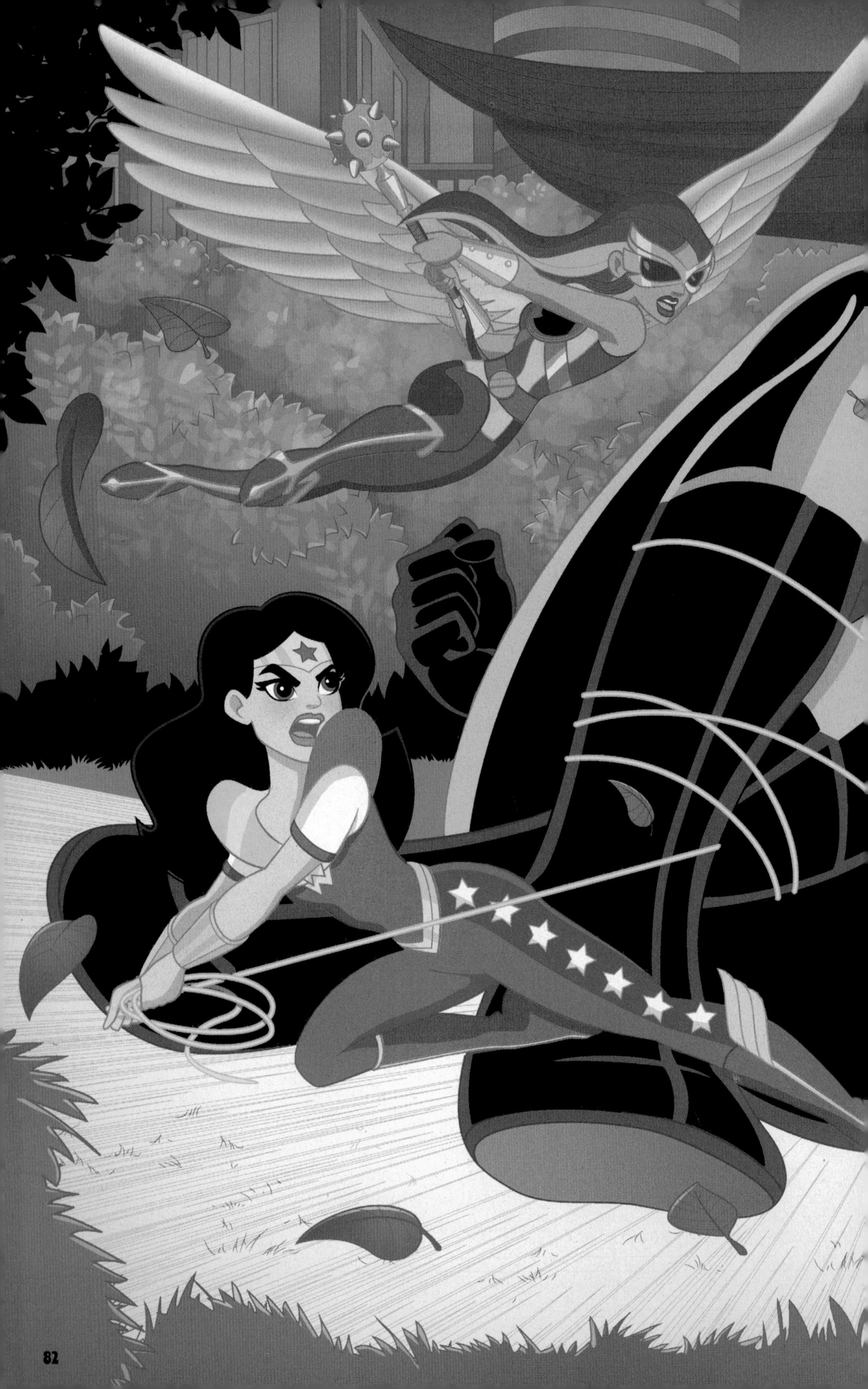

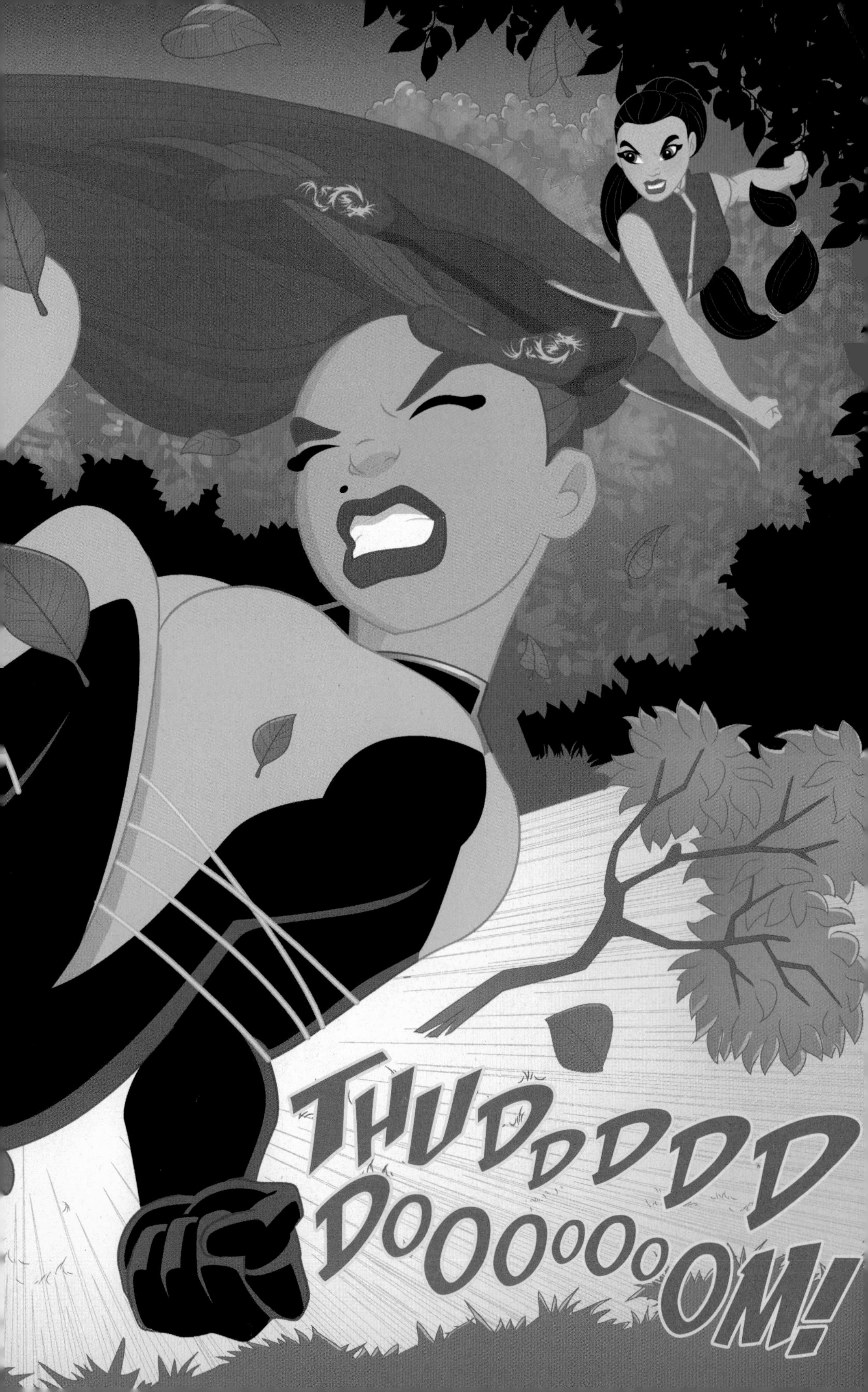
THUDDDDD
DOOOOOOOM!

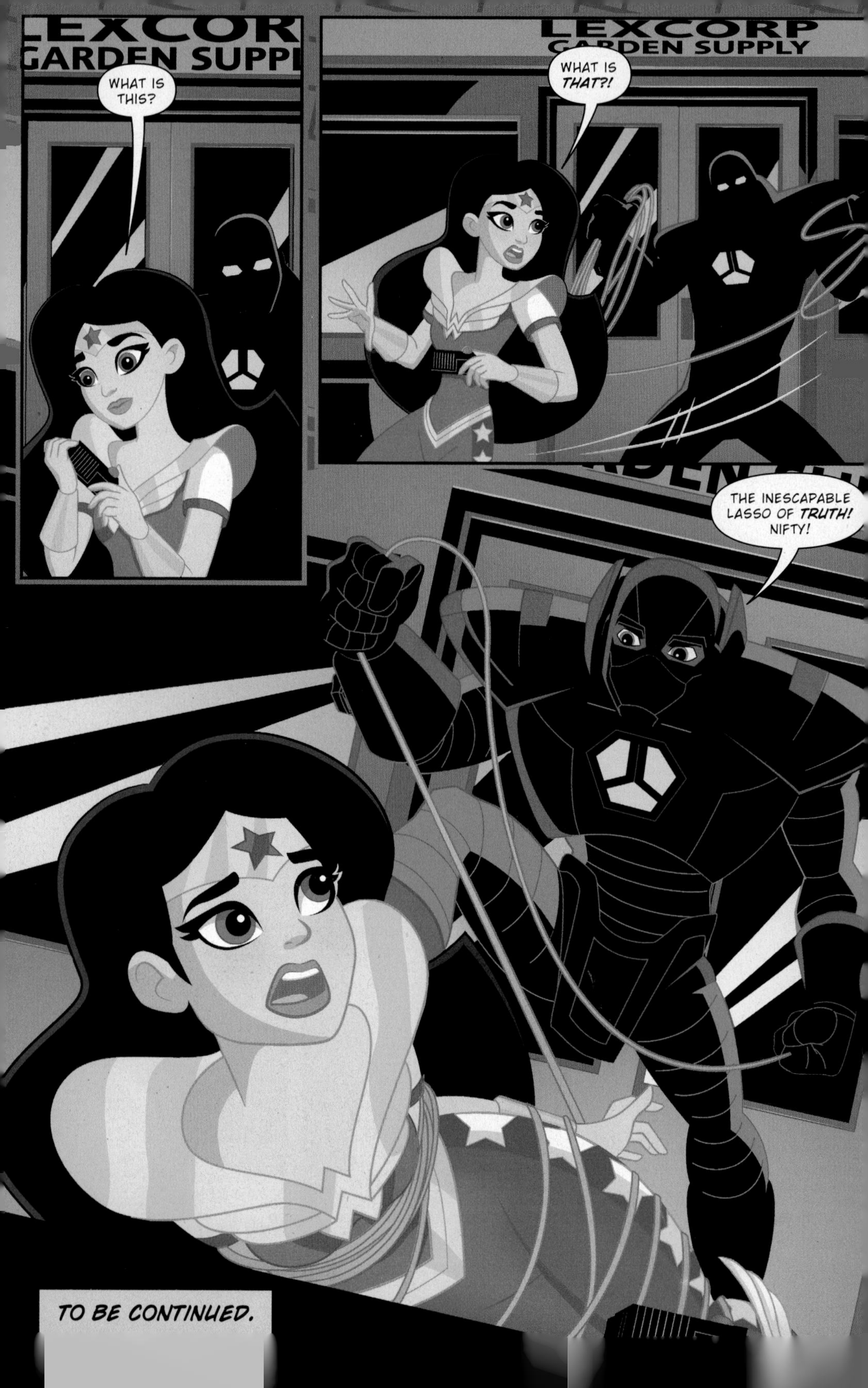
LEXCORP GARDEN SUPPLY
WHAT IS THIS?
LEXCORP GARDEN SUPPLY
WHAT IS THAT?!
THE INESCAPABLE LASSO OF TRUTH! NIFTY!
TO BE CONTINUED.

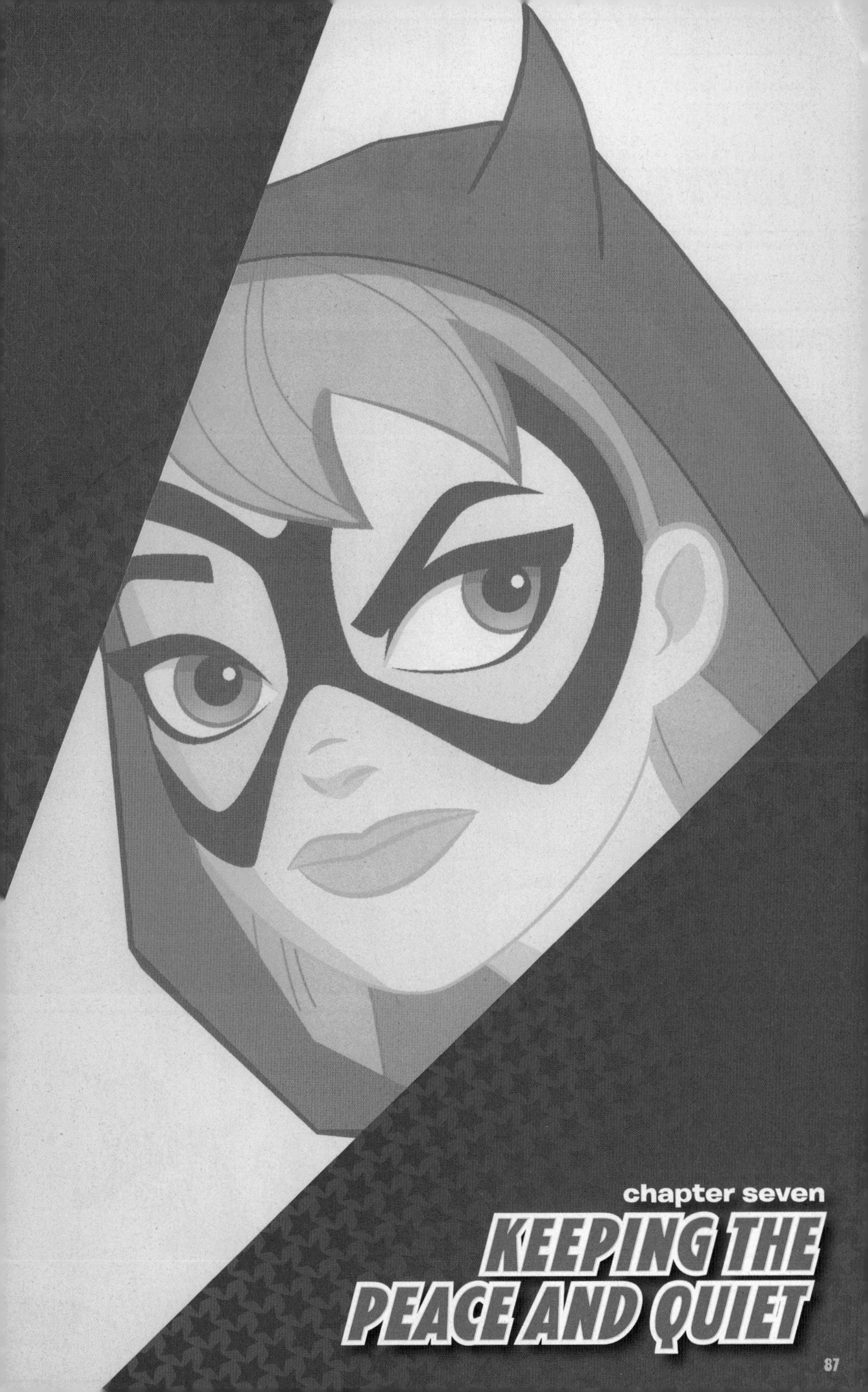

chapter seven

KEEPING THE PEACE AND QUIET

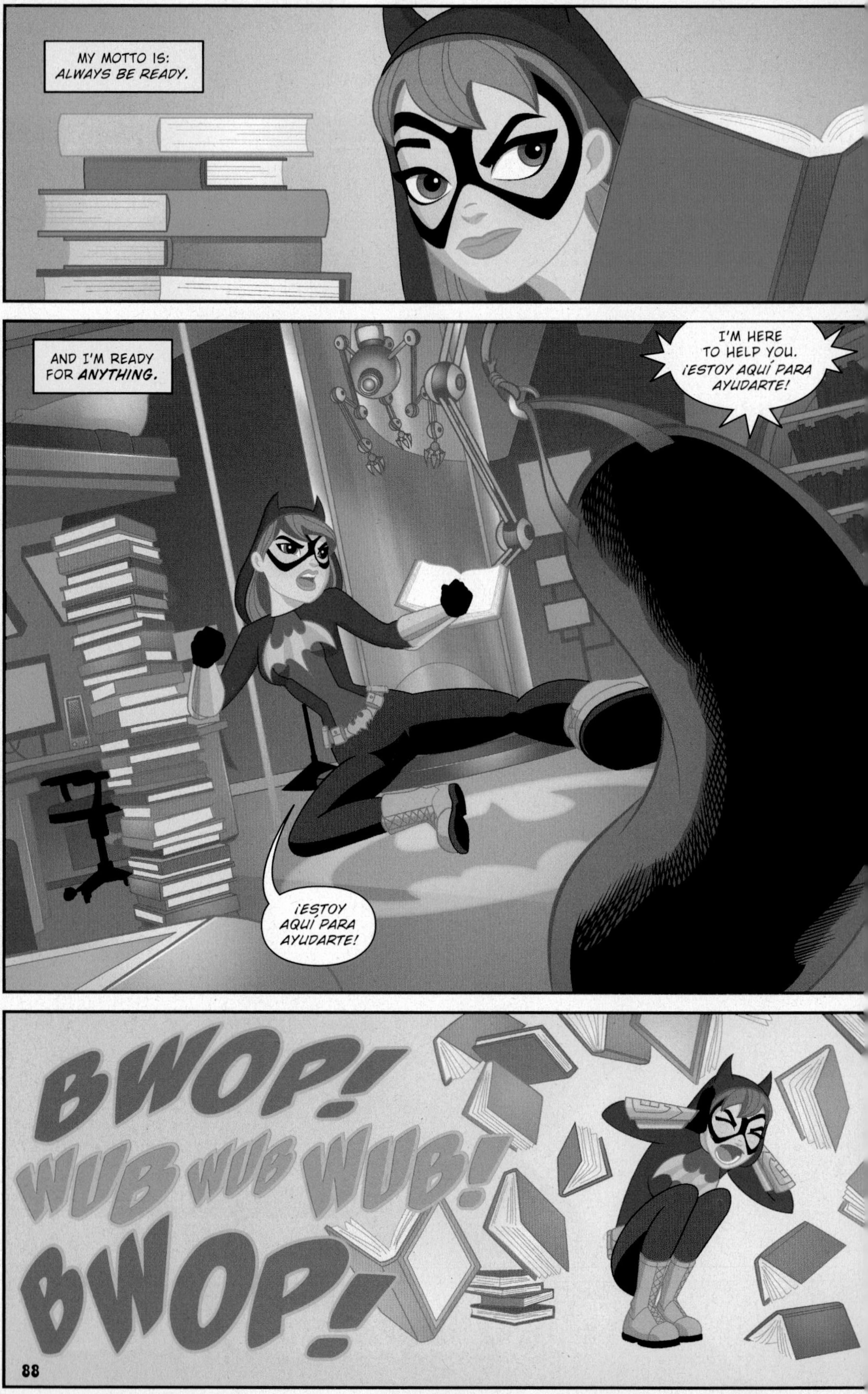

MY MOTTO IS: ALWAYS BE READY.
AND I'M READY FOR ANYTHING.
I'M HERE TO HELP YOU. ¡ESTOY AQUÍ PARA AYUDARTE!
¡ESTOY AQUÍ PARA AYUDARTE!
BWOP! WUB WUB WUB! BWOP!

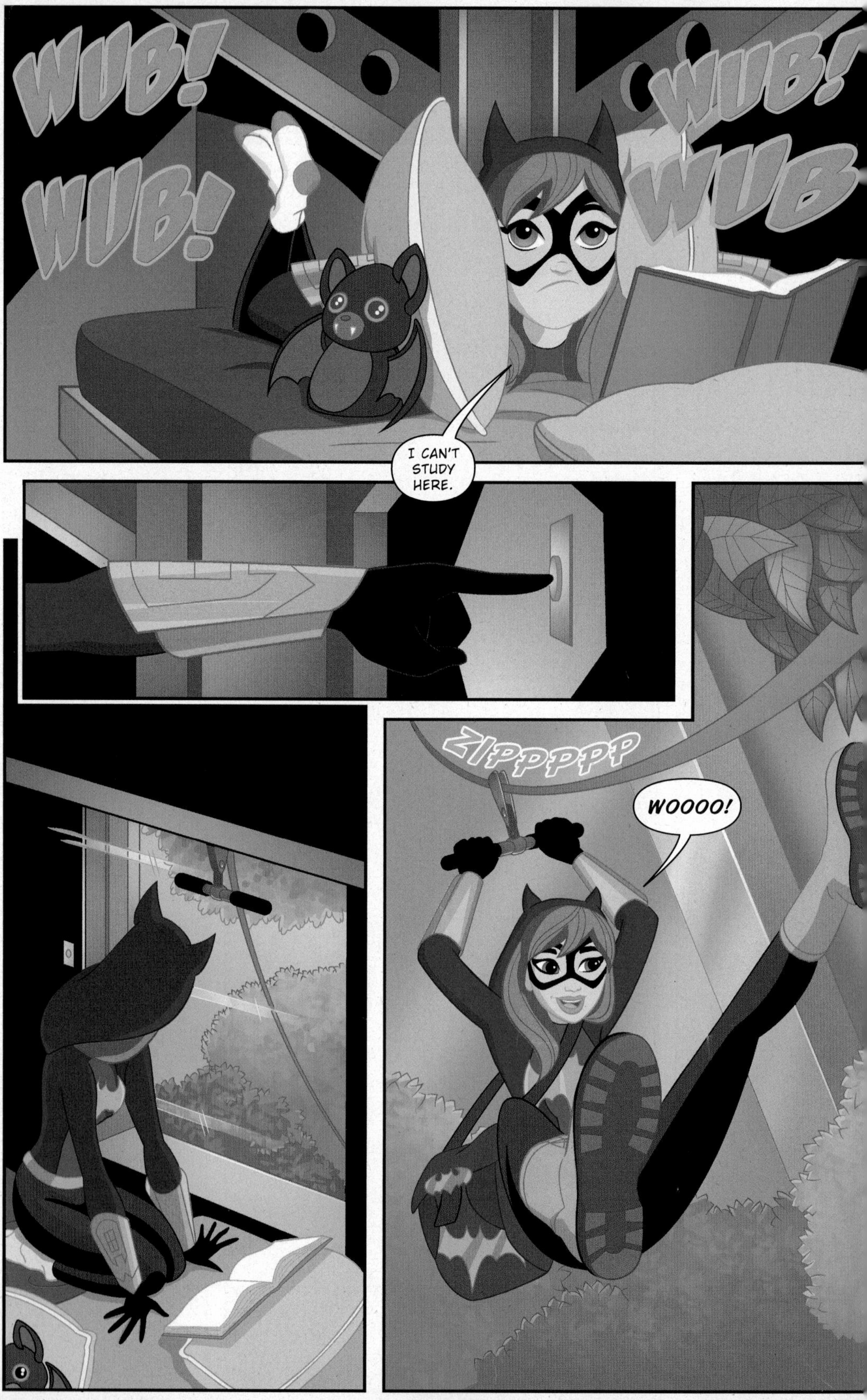
WUB!
WUB!
WUB!
WUB
I CAN'T STUDY HERE.
ZIPPPPP
WOOOO!

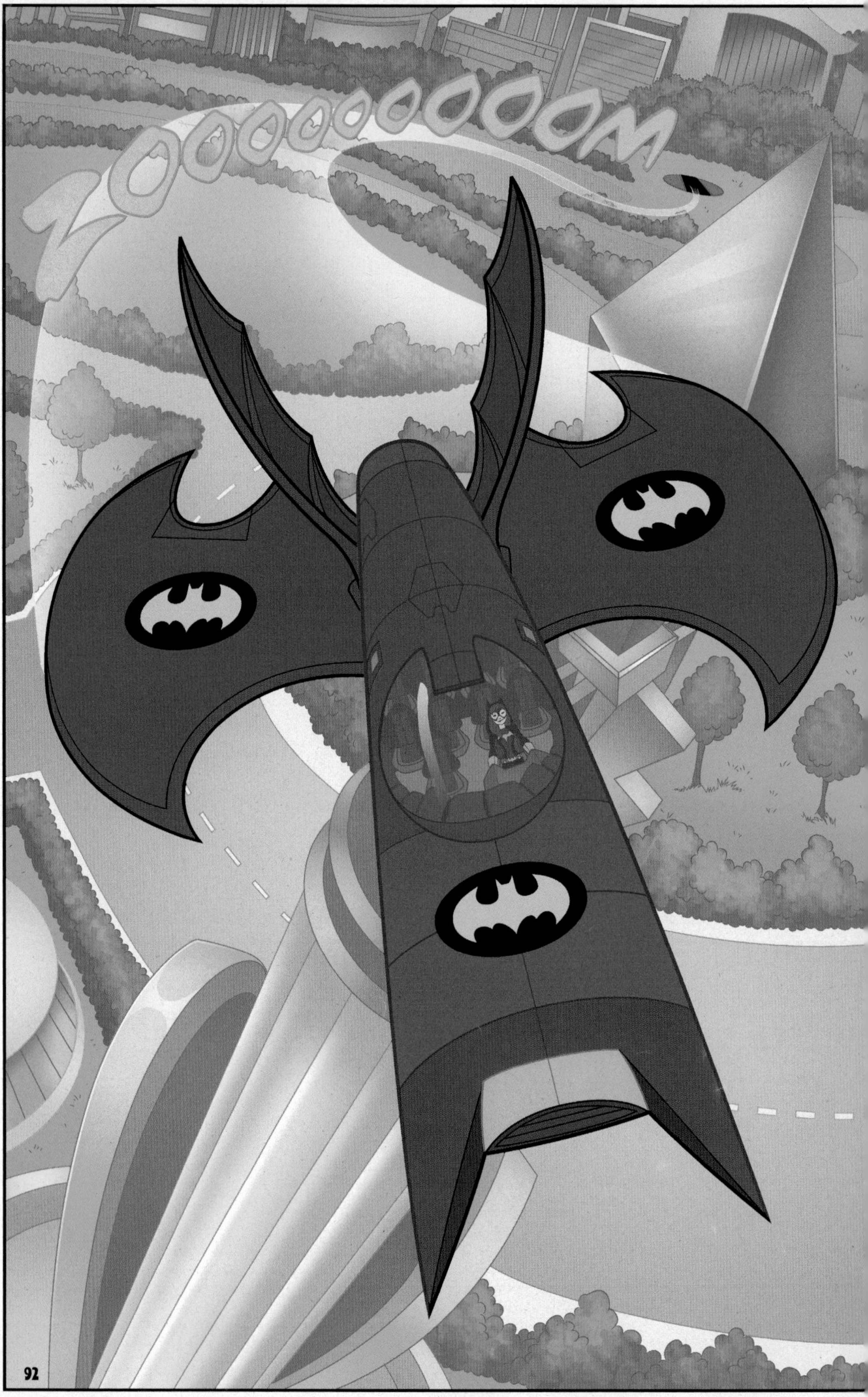
ZOOOOOOOOOM

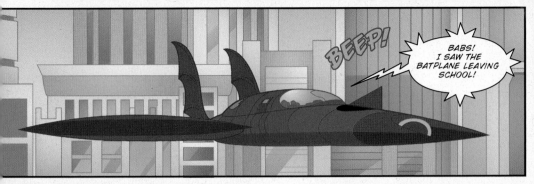

BEEP!

BABS! I SAW THE BATPLANE LEAVING SCHOOL!

WHY AREN'T YOU STUDYING?

I'M *TRYING* TO, DAD!

IT WAS *TOO LOUD* THERE!

"BUT DON'T WORRY. I'M HEADED TO THE PERFECT STUDY SPOT!"

WELCOME, BATGIRL.

TO--

93

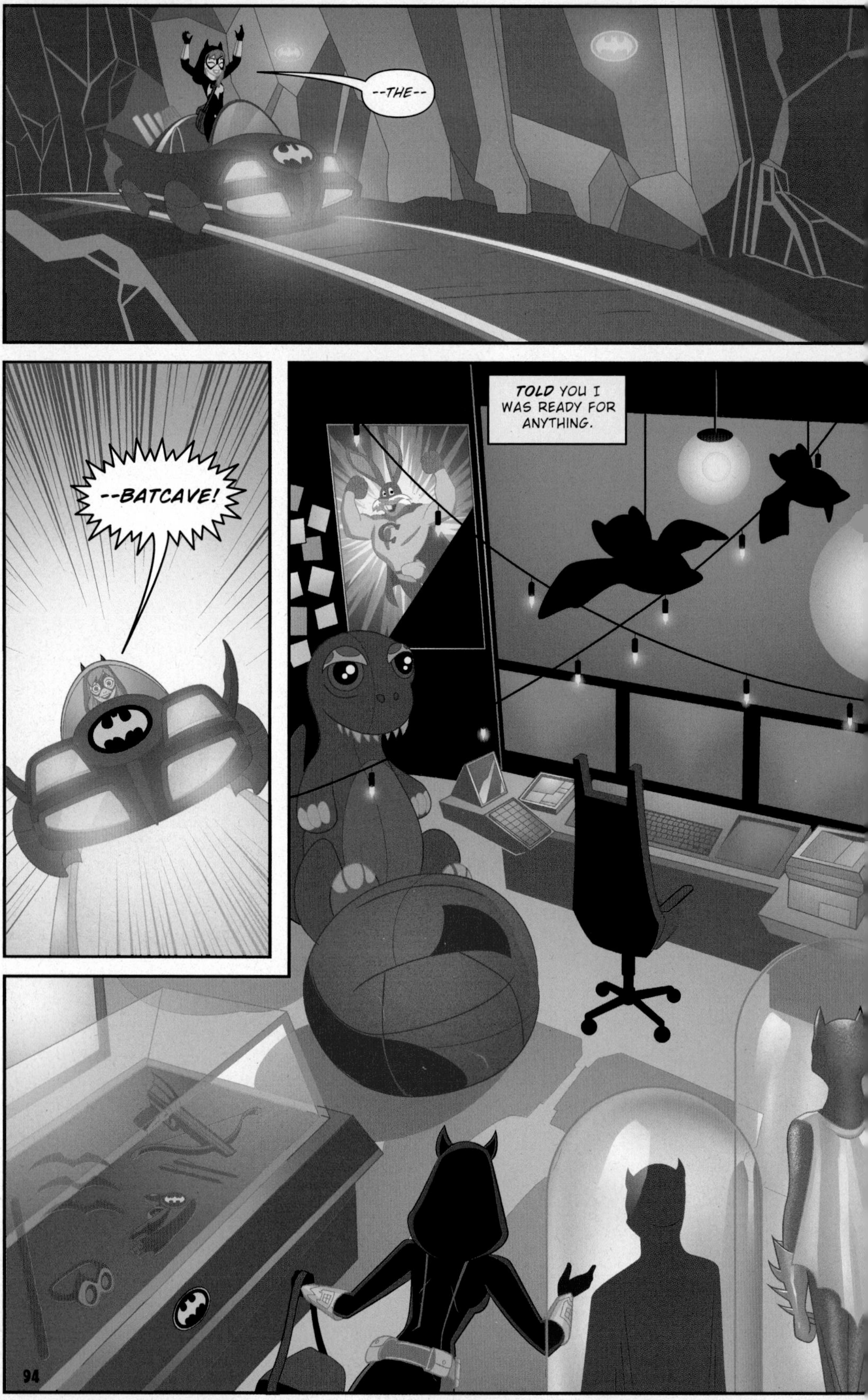
--THE--
--BATCAVE!
TOLD YOU I WAS READY FOR ANYTHING.

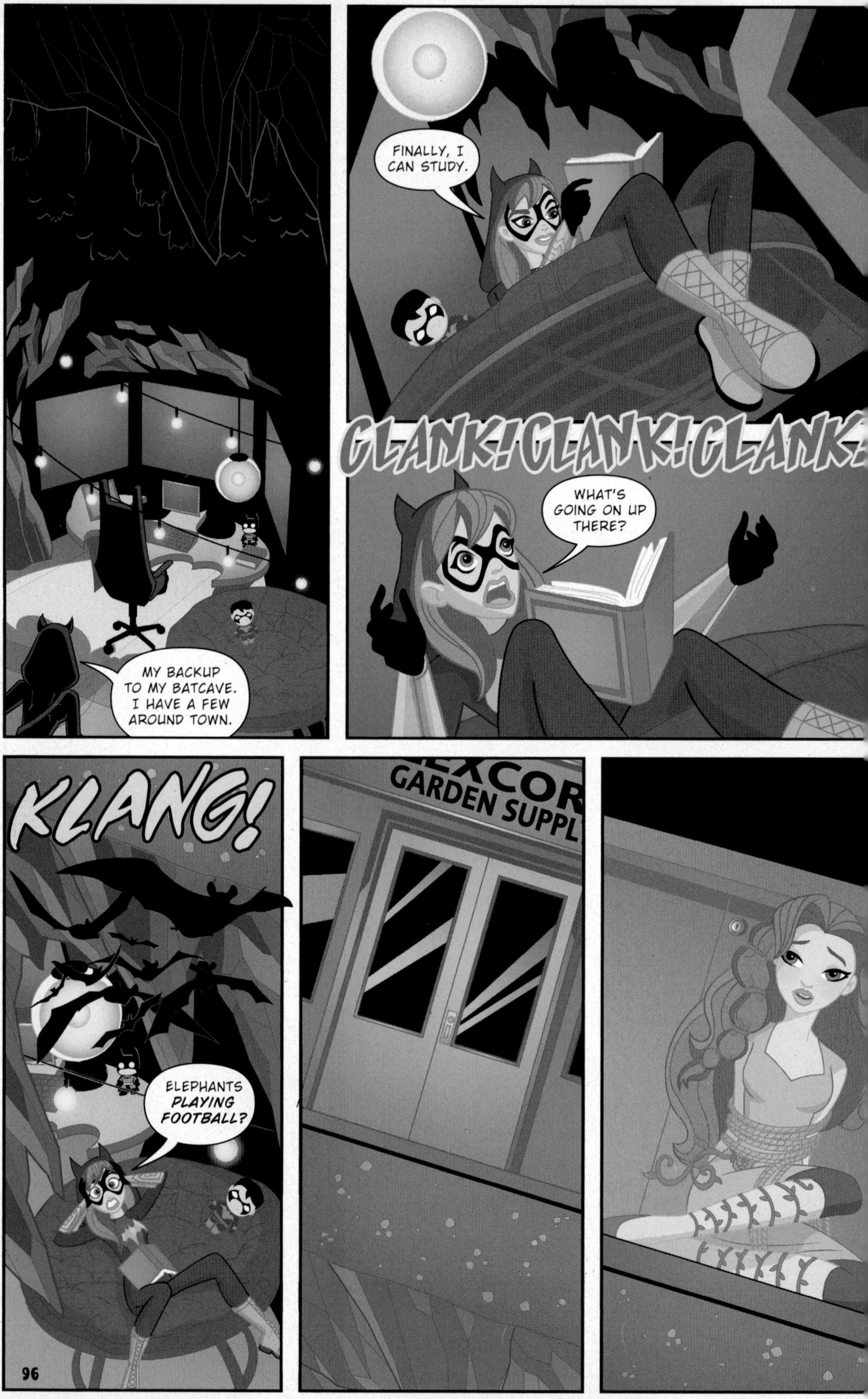
MY BACKUP TO MY BATCAVE. I HAVE A FEW AROUND TOWN.
FINALLY, I CAN STUDY.
CLANK! CLANK! CLANK!
WHAT'S GOING ON UP THERE?
KLANG!
ELEPHANTS PLAYING FOOTBALL?
EXCOR GARDEN SUPPL

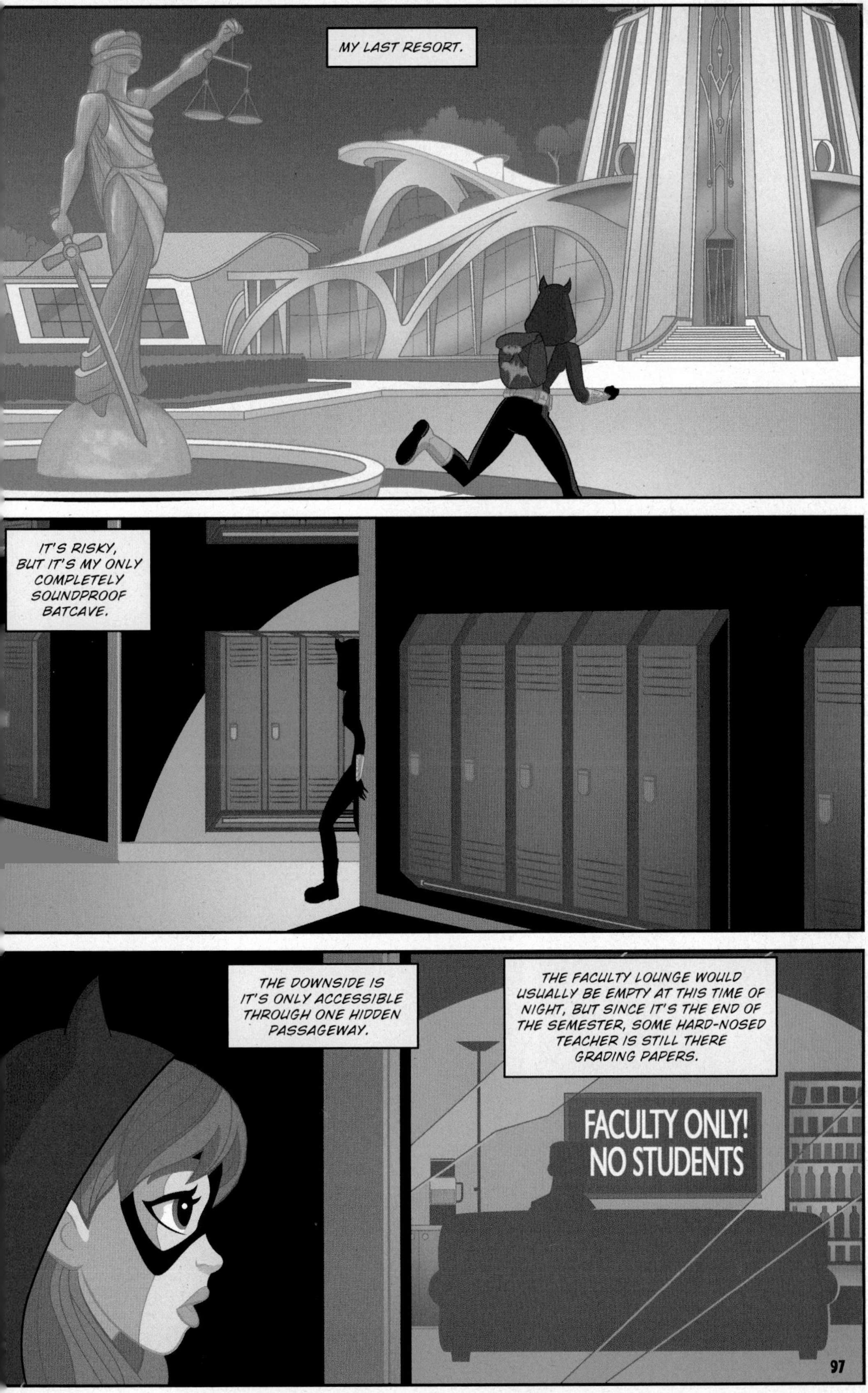
MY LAST RESORT.
IT'S RISKY, BUT IT'S MY ONLY COMPLETELY SOUNDPROOF BATCAVE.
THE DOWNSIDE IS IT'S ONLY ACCESSIBLE THROUGH ONE HIDDEN PASSAGEWAY.
THE FACULTY LOUNGE WOULD USUALLY BE EMPTY AT THIS TIME OF NIGHT, BUT SINCE IT'S THE END OF THE SEMESTER, SOME HARD-NOSED TEACHER IS STILL THERE GRADING PAPERS.
FACULTY ONLY! NO STUDENTS

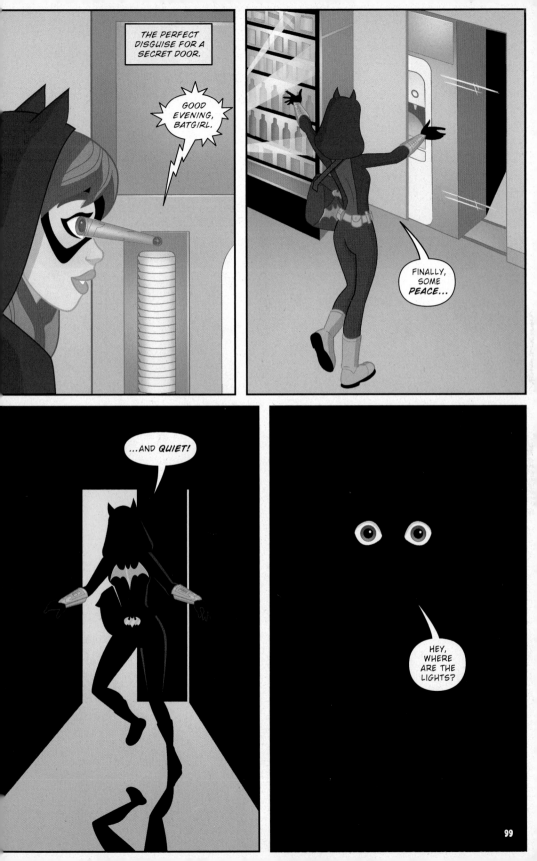

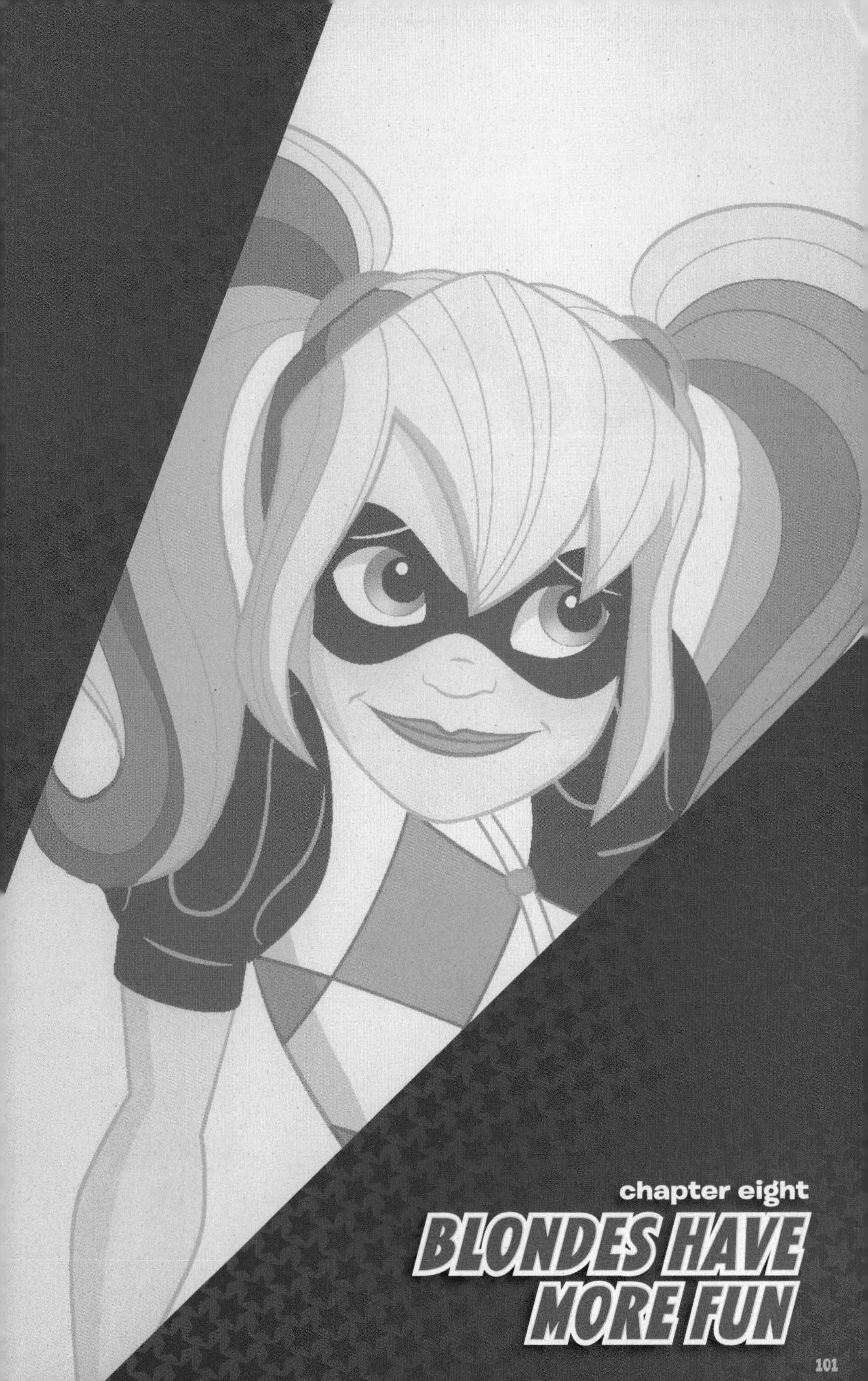

chapter eight

BLONDES HAVE MORE FUN

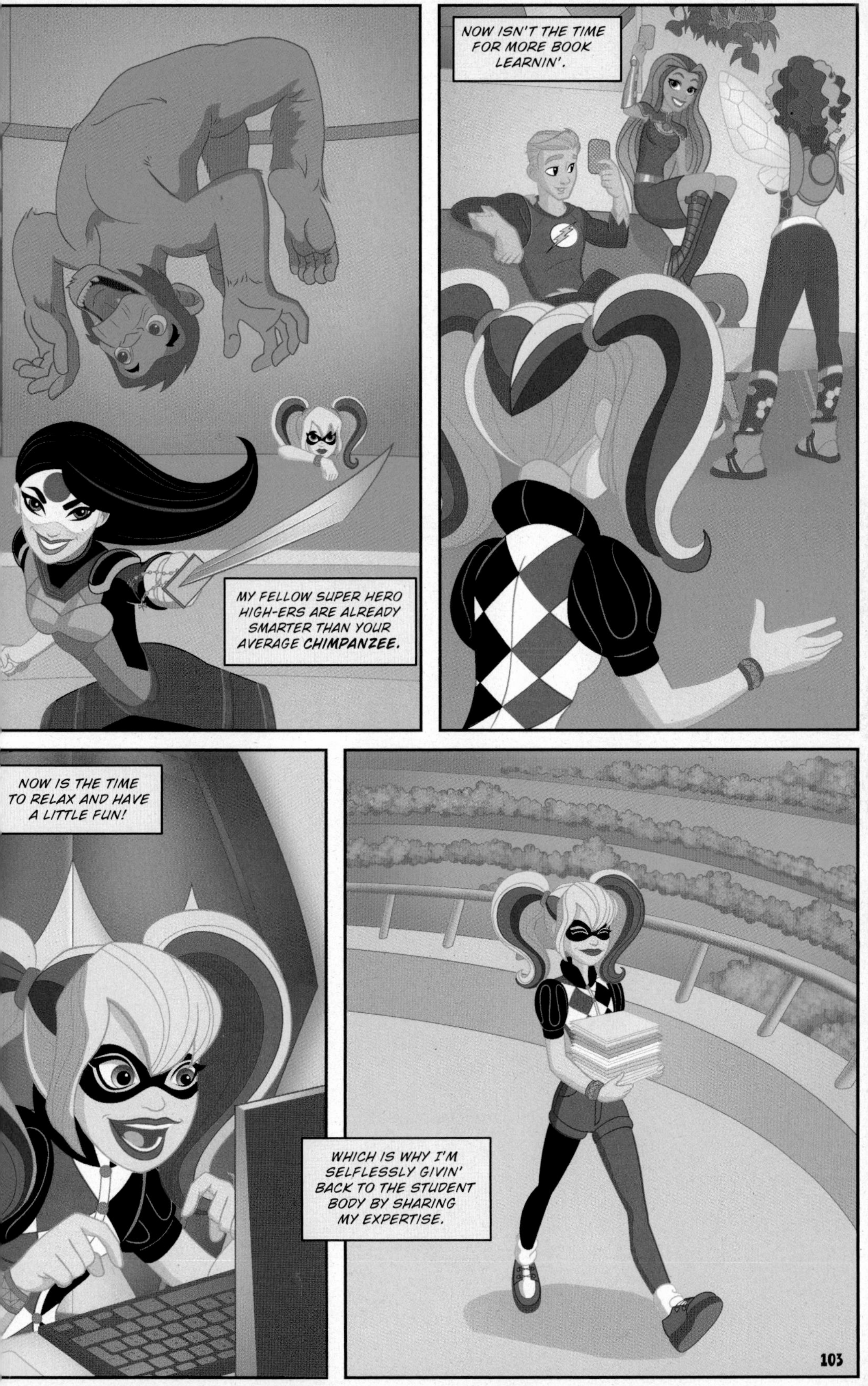
MY FELLOW SUPER HERO HIGH-ERS ARE ALREADY SMARTER THAN YOUR AVERAGE **CHIMPANZEE.**
NOW ISN'T THE TIME FOR MORE BOOK LEARNIN'.
NOW IS THE TIME TO RELAX AND HAVE A LITTLE FUN!
WHICH IS WHY I'M SELFLESSLY GIVIN' BACK TO THE STUDENT BODY BY SHARING MY EXPERTISE.

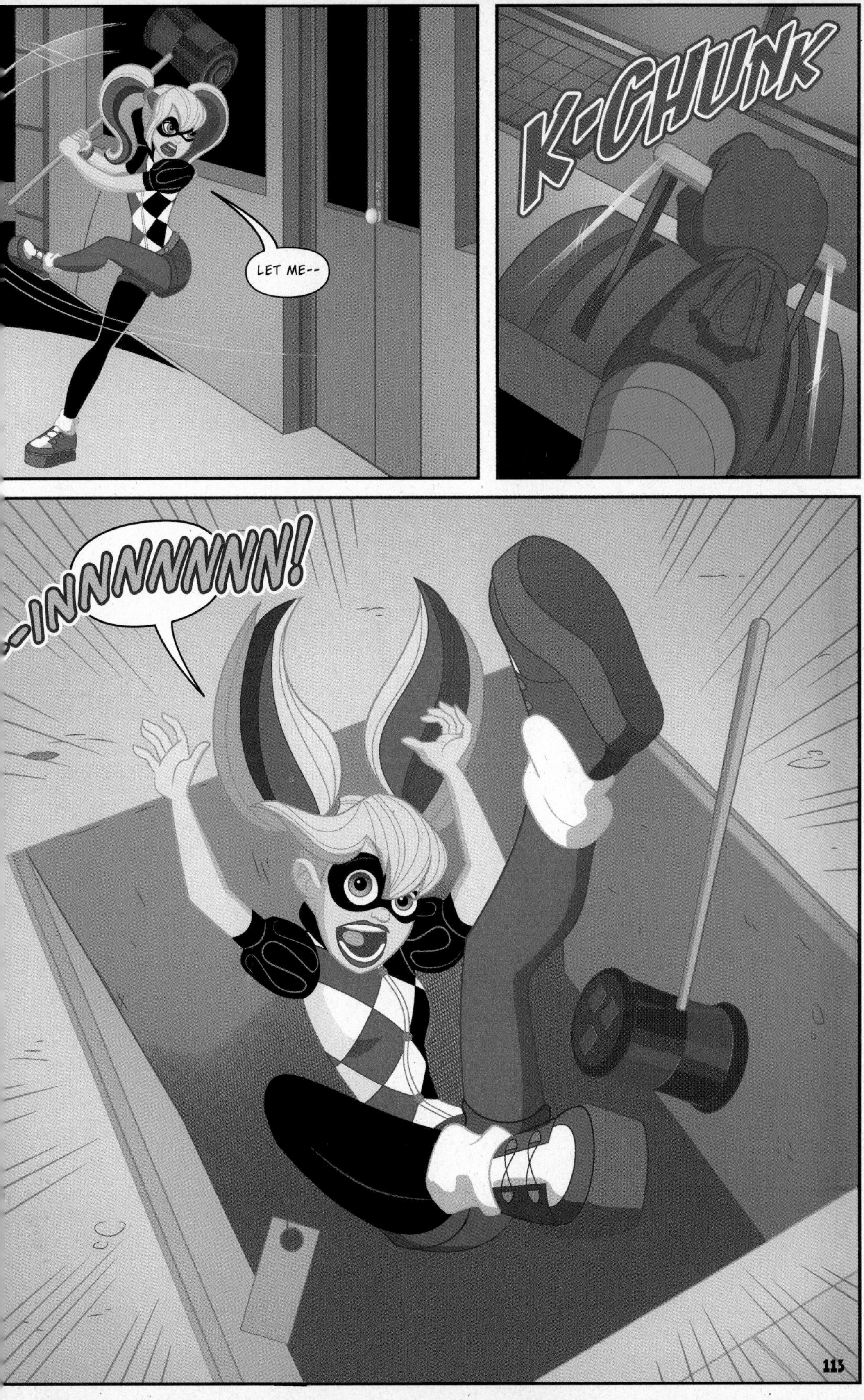
LET ME--
K-CHUNK
-INNNNNNN!

TO BE CONCLUDED.

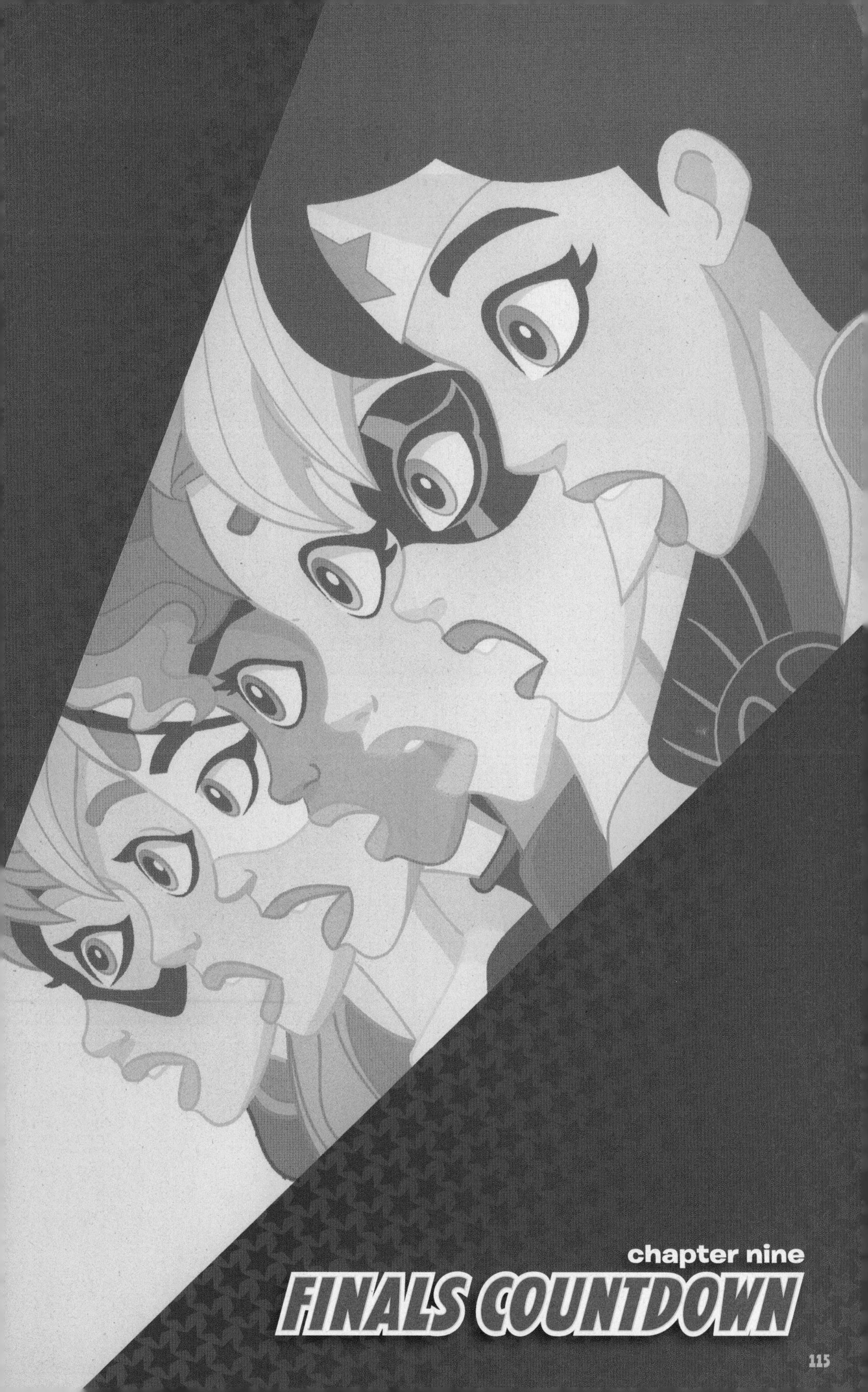

chapter nine

FINALS COUNTDOWN

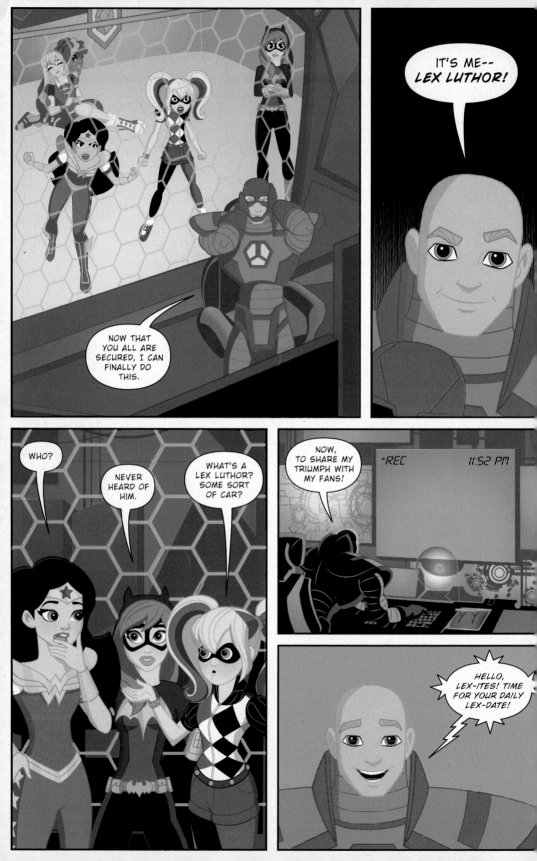

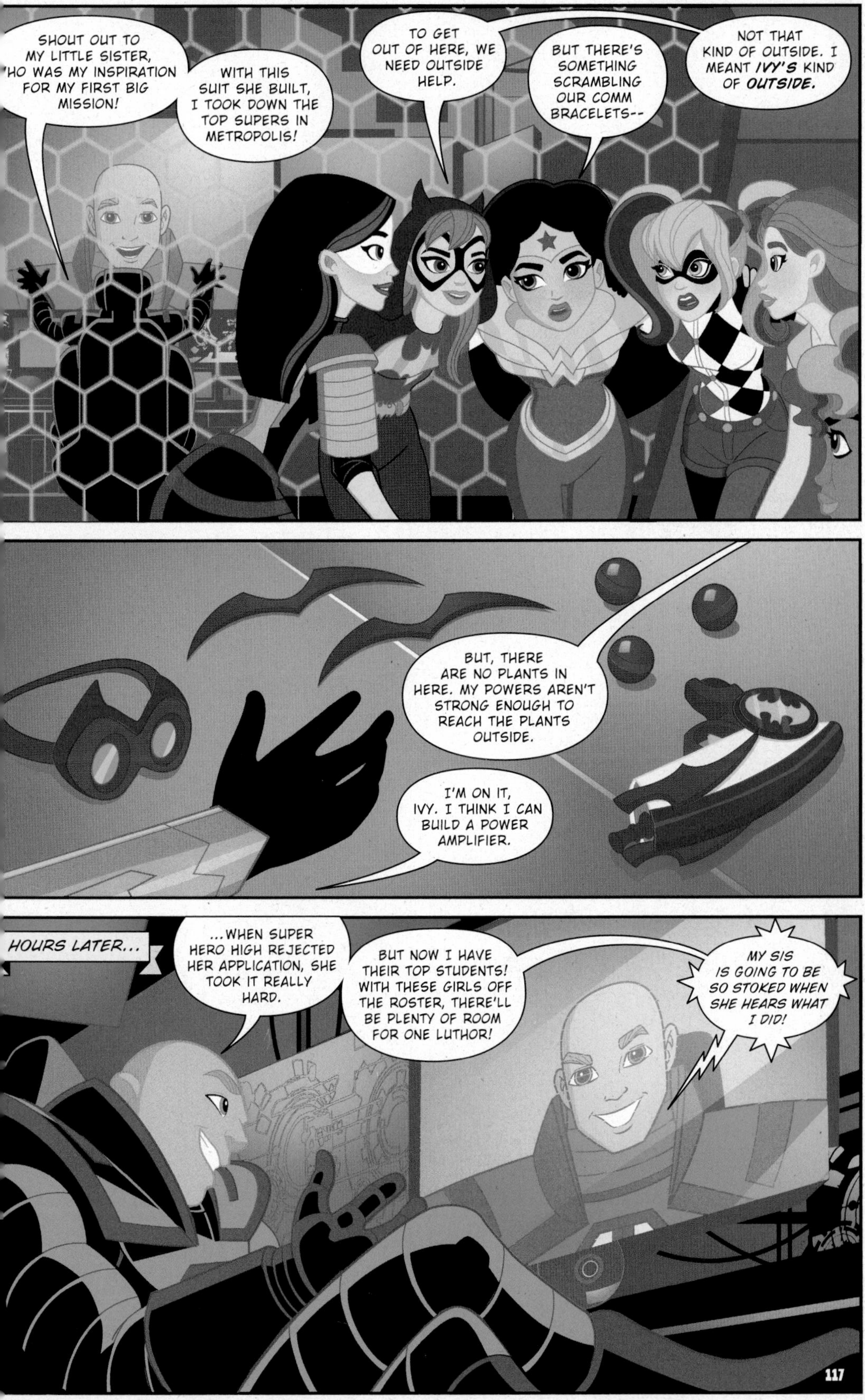
SHOUT OUT TO MY LITTLE SISTER, WHO WAS MY INSPIRATION FOR MY FIRST BIG MISSION!
WITH THIS SUIT SHE BUILT, I TOOK DOWN THE TOP SUPERS IN METROPOLIS!
TO GET OUT OF HERE, WE NEED OUTSIDE HELP.
BUT THERE'S SOMETHING SCRAMBLING OUR COMM BRACELETS--
NOT THAT KIND OF OUTSIDE. I MEANT IVY'S KIND OF OUTSIDE.
BUT, THERE ARE NO PLANTS IN HERE. MY POWERS AREN'T STRONG ENOUGH TO REACH THE PLANTS OUTSIDE.
I'M ON IT, IVY. I THINK I CAN BUILD A POWER AMPLIFIER.
HOURS LATER...
...WHEN SUPER HERO HIGH REJECTED HER APPLICATION, SHE TOOK IT REALLY HARD.
BUT NOW I HAVE THEIR TOP STUDENTS! WITH THESE GIRLS OFF THE ROSTER, THERE'LL BE PLENTY OF ROOM FOR ONE LUTHOR!
MY SIS IS GOING TO BE SO STOKED WHEN SHE HEARS WHAT I DID!

THE END.

about the

AUTHOR

Shea Fontana is a writer for film, television, and graphic novels. Her credits include *DC Super Hero Girls* animated shorts, television specials, and movies, *Dorothy and the Wonders of Oz*, *Doc McStuffins*, *The 7D*, *Whisker Haven Tales with the Palace Pets*, *Disney on Ice*, and the feature film *Crowning Jules*. She lives in sunny Los Angeles where she enjoys playing roller derby, hiking, hanging out with her dog, Moxie, and changing her hair color. ★

about the

COLORIST

Monica Kubina has colored countless comics, including super hero series, manga titles, kids comics, and science fiction stories. She's colored *Phineas and Ferb*, *SpongeBob*, *THE 99*, and *Star Wars*. Monica's favorite activities are bike riding and going to museums with her husband and two young sons. ★

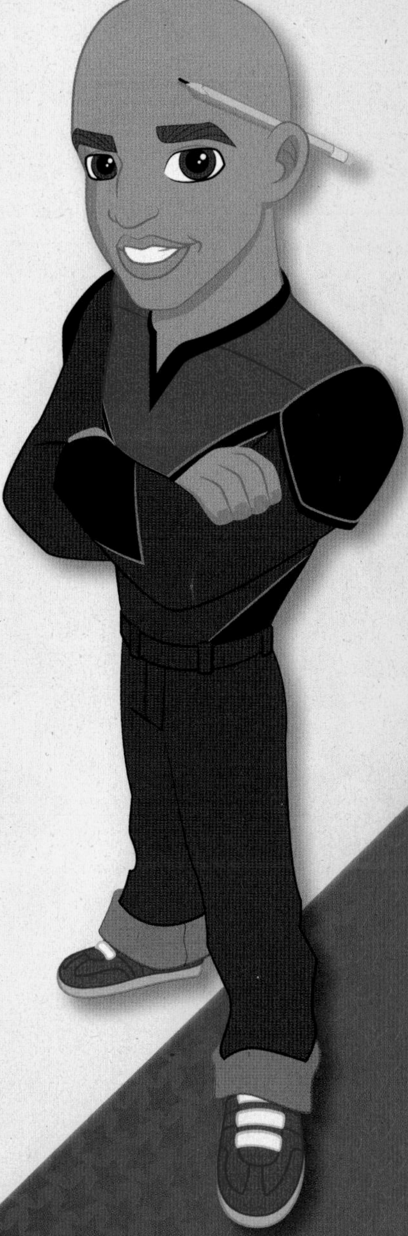

about the
ARTIST

Yancey Labat got his start at Marvel Comics before moving on to illustrate children's books from *Hello Kitty* to *Peanuts* for Scholastic, as well as books for Chronicle Books, ABC Mouse, and others. His book *How Many Jellybeans?* with writer Andrea Menotti won the 2013 Cook Prize for best STEM (Science, Technology, Education, Math) picture book from Bank Street College of Education. He has two super hero girls of his own and lives in Cupertino, California. ★

about the
LETTERER

Janice Chiang has lettered *Archie, Barbie, Punisher* and many more. She was the first woman to win the Comic Buyer's Guide Fan Awards for Best Letterer (2011). She likes weight training, hiking, baking, gardening, and traveling. ★

DC SUPER HERO GIRLS

www.**dcsuperherogirls**.com

Follow the adventure:

Get to know the **SUPER HEROES**
of Metropolis and watch all-new
animated content online

ALWAYS ASK YOUR PARENTS BEFORE GOING ONLINE

GET YOUR CAPE ON.

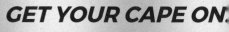